INSTRUCTOR'S MANUAL

Inside fashion DESIGN

FIFTH EDITION

Sharon Lee Tate

PEARSON
Prentice Hall

Upper Saddle River, New Jersey 07458

Pearson Prentice Hall™ is a trademark of Pearson Education, Inc.
Pearson® is a registered trademark of Pearson plc
Prentice Hall® is a registered trademark of Pearson Education, Inc.

Pearson Education LTD.
Pearson Education Singapore, Pte. Ltd
Pearson Education, Canada, Ltd
Pearson Education–Japan
Pearson Education Australia PTY, Limited
Pearson Education North Asia Ltd
Pearson Educaçion de Mexico, S.A. de C.V.
Pearson Education Malaysia, Pte. Ltd

10 9 8 7 6 5 4 3 2 1
ISBN 0-13-112887-6

INSIDE FASHION DESIGN, 5th edition

CONTENTS

READINGS FROM FASHION FORWARD: *Assessing the Future of Apparel Manufacturing in Los Angeles County*

OBJECTIVES

Inside Fashion Design, 5th Edition, is written as a foundation textbook for students interested in careers as apparel designers, manufacturers, retailers, contractors, and in fashion support industries. The integration of business, manufacturing and creative aspects of product development form the core of the textbook. Instructors can use *Inside Fashion Design* to teach a wide variety of courses typically found in college and university fashion design and merchandising programs.

The text contains the core material. The manual presents more complex and detailed instructor's information, problem solving exercises, field trips, test questions, and creative problems that can be modified for specific courses. Creative graphic projects have been created for design students. Both merchandising and design students benefit from business and trend research projects. General fashion problems are tailored for first-time fashion students. All projects have been tested in a classroom.

Encourage students to read the textbook before coming to class. Test them on vocabulary or require responses to the chapter questions at the beginning of a class period to ensure they are completing the reading assignments. Use the text as a springboard to introduce creative problems and supplemental teaching information.

Reading from the textbook in class is deadly. Avoid it at all costs. Tell the students how the course will be taught from the beginning, what they are going to do most of the time and what will be expected of them. Encourage them to become critical thinkers by requiring them to actively use the subject, not memorize information by rote. Instead, require them to internalize the information by using it actively in class to solve problems and class assignments. Teach students to think as if they were fashion professionals.

An excellent method of checking to see if students have completed a reading assignment is a crossword puzzle based on the homework reading assignment. Students complete the puzzle during the first ten minutes of class. Simple computer software programs are available that allow you to design crossword puzzles to effectively check if students have read the material. These exercises diversify graded assignments and validate attendance as well.

Use engaging lectures by writing each student's name on a flash card. Shuffle through the cards, calling on students at random as their names come up to elaborate or illustrate points in the text. Involve every student in the class, encouraging active listening because they can expect to be called on. Welcome "deep learning" questions by encouraging students to internalize responses to questions and create solutions to problems.

Train your students to use the information they have read to solve creative or business problems. Using information instead of listening to an instructor repeat the reading assignment is a very effective way to learn the material. Use lectures to reinforce the information with a regional perspective that fits your locale.

GENERAL FASHION PROBLEMS

General problems are suitable for all fashion students planning a career in some aspect of the fashion industry that does not require drawing skills. The primary focus is developing a taste level, selecting appropriate solutions to problems, developing a vocabulary, researching fashion trends, fabric and trim information, career direction, and merchandising skills. These problems rely on the "real life fashion laboratory" provided by retail apparel stores, regional wholesale markets, and fabric producers.

Discuss the basic components of problem solving with your students:

- Clearly define the goals and limitations of the situation
- Ask questions
- Gather data and information
- Make inferences about the data
- Trace implications
- Transform the data or create a solution that addresses all aspects of the problem

CREATIVE DESIGN PROBLEMS

Creative exercises and problems allow students with the ability to draw and design to develop croquis, storyboards and fashion plates appropriate for a portfolio. Illustration skills, creativity, and synthesis are stressed in each exercise. Many of the creative problems require integrating design solutions with commercial business issues.

MERCHANDISING PROBLEMS

Students planning to become buyers, retailers, fashion coordinators, advertising copywriters, art directors, or who are entering other fashion careers that do not require drawing skills are presented with problems that involve research, observation, and synthesis of ideas from printed material and store research. Little or no sketching is required to successfully complete these exercises.

Inside Fashion Design can also be used as a foundation text for advanced design and patternmaking courses. Advanced creative projects are presented when appropriate. Many of the basic design projects can be used in advanced courses by requiring students to drape, make a pattern and construct a garment based on a story board, illustration, or croquis. Students should also be encouraged to tackle some of the more elaborate projects as a team.

SUPPLEMENTARY TEACHING INFORMATION

Some chapters include additional technical information and teaching aids as optional lectures to be used at the discretion of the instructor. Companion reference and textbooks are also mentioned, but the range of fashion textbooks and consumer publications is so diverse and ever changing that the suggested reference lists should not be construed as a complete bibliography.

FIELD TRIP AND GUEST LECTURE RECOMMENDATIONS

These are most practical for schools located in an apparel-producing center. When possible, field trips and guest lecturers for the non-apparel producing locations are also included. Virtual field trips and lectures are available via the Internet and distance learning technology. Consider linking with community colleges and universities with specialized fashion, textile, and apparel business programs using distance learning and e-links.

TEST AND QUIZ QUESTIONS

Test questions are included for each chapter. Team these with vocabulary lists included at the end of each chapter. Assign students the short responses to the study questions at the end of each chapter.

No true/false or multiple-choice questions are provided. I feel the power of the written word is very strong and there is a tendency to retain an incorrect statement presented as a test question. This is particularly true for students speaking English as a second language. I prefer to take a positive approach and ask for a response from the student. Develop your own short essay questions to challenge students to provide a literate response. Copy diagrams from the text and "white-out" labels. Test students on the names and parts of garments. Reference page numbers are provided instead of answers so instructors can refer to the text for the appropriate response.

Tests are the best way of assessing if students have mastered basic vocabulary, concepts and definitions. Creative problems and written solutions to problems are much more indicative of how students have internalized the information.

PRESENTING THE PROBLEMS OR EXERCISES

1. Assign the chapter as outside reading and validate student performance with a short quiz or crossword puzzle.

2. Lecture on the principles in the text using these techniques:
    a. customize information for a specific region
    b. show examples of garments, trims, research material and so forth to connect written concepts with visual examples. Slides or Internet sites that display designer shows or fashion trends are powerful examples to stimulate discussion.
    c. use Power Point or slide presentations of period clothing to discuss silhouettes and details or styling principles
    d. demonstrate construction and draping techniques when appropriate

3.   Present a homework assignment beginning with specific criteria for presenting the student's solution. Learning to follow directions is part of the expected outcome. Limit and define the response you would like from each student. If necessary, divide the merchandising and design students into two groups with different outcomes for the same project. For example, you may require the design students to sketch solutions and merchandising students to cut photos from magazines. Early projects may be more structured than later ones.

   a. require a specific size board to present the project
   b. define the rendering and presentation methods
   c. mention how many designs or solutions are required
   d. be specific about due dates and grade late projects by deducting points or grades

4.   Reserve time to work with individuals in class. Most projects have no single best answer and should stimulate a creative and unique solution. For this reason it is important to work with each student. Longer projects should be done in several phases

   Require preliminary sketches or fabric groups. Make editing and changes part of the process, because this is typical of the real world. Require that some work be done in class if time permits. Many students cannot work outside of a sheltered environment and this is unrealistic in the real world, plus, you can check to see if the work is the student's own.

5.   Final evaluations and grading can be done in several ways. It is vital for the instructor to give specific feedback to students when complicated creative or research projects are evaluated. Here are some techniques for grading:

   a. attach tracing paper to a sketch or illustration with a small piece of masking tape. Make suggestions, notes and corrective drawings on the tracing paper so the project remains untouched.
   b. stress professionalism by asking students to consider each project as a part of their portfolio by asking the question, "Would you like a future employer to judge you with this piece of work?"
   c. peer reviews are positive experiences when the instructor establishes specific criteria and guides the critique. Ask questions like:

      Were directions followed? Does the presentation or sketching technique convey the designer's ideas clearly? Is the garment appropriate for the customer, price range, and category? Are garments appropriate for a specific retailer or type of store?

6. More sophisticated projects may be evaluated by professionals. Invite a designer, buyer, merchant, or other knowledgeable individual to class to critique the projects. This person should be thoroughly briefed on the criteria and requirements of the assignment. The professional may want to assist setting up the requirements before the project is assigned. The guest may want to play the part of an employer, judging the students by their graphic work as this is the typical way a designer is selected in industry. The professional may spot a promising person during his/her visit and become a valuable contact for placing graduates on a job.

THE CREATIVE DESIGN PROBLEM

Collect scrap (reference photographs and sketches) from fashion sources that relate to specific projects. Separate them into folders or large envelopes labeled with the title of the project. Add to them whenever you find stimulating material. Be constantly on the lookout for books and articles that suggest other creative problems. Use your collection of reference material to guide and inspire your students to collect scrap for their personal reference. Encourage them to bring their collections to school to stimulate ideas for projects completed in class.

Research should be an important component of each design project. Design reports, foreign fashion magazines, a personal sketchbook of retail "bodies," period clothing, old magazines, and books are all important stimuli for a designer. Teach your students to collect information as an important part of every project.

Assign short-term assignments due in one class period. Many students complain about having to do an assignment completely in class but this situation is typical of industry. A designer is often pressured to come up with an idea, design, or the solution to a problem on the spot.

Date your files so you can remember when students were last assigned a specific project. Take notes on how effective each project is. This information is particularly important for the teacher who has the same students in many courses. Start your scrap collection and library as soon as possible. Discard projects that do not work for your students and constantly add new themes.

Some projects suggested in this manual are:

1. quilts as garments or fabric print inspiration
2. adult sleepwear and robes
3. bridal dresses (collect historical photos and encourage discussion on the social implications of weddings as well as design trends.)
4. oriental inspiration (use Japanese or Chinese reference material, textiles, folk costumes and art)
5. resort and swimwear
6. white on white themes

7. uniforms (expand from the obvious "service" uniforms to specific categories including stewardesses, banks, theme restaurants, theme parks and so forth)
8. ruffles
9. children's wear
10. men's spectator sportswear
11. men's active sportswear for a specific sport
12. men's suits
13. plus size women's wear
14. fabric print and trim combos
15. sweaters of many types
16. clothing inspired by ethnic costumes
17. museum shows as inspiration
18. active sportswear for men and women
19. coats, suits and rainwear
20. sheets as garments
21. denim
22. lace
23. figure problems for specific individuals
24. costuming a fictional character
25. using a room interior as inspiration for a garment

SUGGESTED GRADING METHODS

In a career-oriented course, students will have a measure of industry reality if the instructor grades by the "wage" method. To do this, the instructor decides on a "fee" for each project. The wage is paid in points or "money." Each project is evaluated to make the grade reflect the time and effort invested by the student. A classroom assignment could be worth five points, a quiz 25 points/dollars, and the mid-term, final, or project could be valued at 200 points/dollars.

The student is "paid" for his project in points or dollars that determine the level of success achieved. An excellent project should receive the maximum number of points possible. A less well-executed project would receive a lower point wage. Late projects should have a 5-to-10% penalty imposed on the final fee paid. To translate the points/dollars to a letter grade, the following guide can be used:

A = 200 to 180 points (the maximum less 10%
B = 179 to 160 points (a reduction of another 10%)
C = 159 to 130 points (a reduction of 15%)
D = 129 to 110 points (a final reduction of 10% from the lowest C)

The grade book should be available to each student who wants to follow his/her progress. Students will soon realize that a missing assignment is disastrous to their final grade. At the end of the semester or quarter, all the wage points should be totaled. Then use the formula above with the

x

total possible points to determine the letter grade from the numerical total. I find this system rewards consistency, and prompt performance, and encourages good work habits in the classroom, because each person knows exactly where s(he) stands.

Students sometimes copy a design exactly. This is cheating. When I find a direct "swipe", I paste a picture of the original work on the student's assignment and return it with a zero grade.

A trick to publicly posting final grades without disclosing student names is to write the last four numbers of the social security number (or student ID number depending on your college identification system) adjacent to the student name. Enter your grades on the roster and make a photocopy, cutting off the student name.

BUILDING A TEST OR QUIZ FROM THE QUESTIONS PROVIDED

A variety of test questions have been provided for each chapter so the instructor can construct a test according to personal preference. I suggest a combination of types of questions. Some should require short answers, and vocabulary definitions, and others should require a longer explanation to compare and contrast two issues or evaluate a process. Writing is a critical skill and should be practiced.

I value testing to determine that a student has absorbed a concept, learned a vocabulary word, or understood a process. Using the information to solve a problem effectively is more important than simply memorizing facts. I urge you to use at least one project in each course so the student is forced to apply the concepts with personal experiments that require envisioning a solution and making decisions based upon what has been learned from the text.

A quiz should be given before the mid-term to acquaint the student with your style of testing.

SCANS SKILLS

The Secretary's Commission on Achieving Necessary Skills (SCANS), was established in 1990 to examine the demands of the work place and to determine whether the current and future workforce is capable of meeting those demands. A year later, the Commission issued its first report to advise the Secretary of Labor on the type and skill levels required for employment and to develop a strategy to disseminate the findings to the nation's schools, businesses, and homes.

This study revealed five competencies that are critical for success backed up by a three-part foundation of basic skills, thinking skills, and personal qualities.

These competencies and skills are listed below because all are relevant to the complicated task of product development, production and sales that are discussed in *Inside Fashion Design, Fifth Edition.* The problems and experiences described in this manual emphasize activities that instructors will develop these competencies and skills as they relate to a career in the fashion industry. Review these with your students and constantly refer to them as you refine your discussion, problems, and field trips.

FIVE COMPETENCIES

Resources: Identifies, organizes, plans, and allocates resources

   A. Time – selects goal-relevant activities, ranks them, and prepares and follows schedules
   B. Money – uses or prepares budgets, makes forecasts, keeps records, and makes adjustments to meet objectives
   C. Materials and Facilities – acquires, stores, allocates and uses space or materials efficiently
   D. Human Resources – assesses skills and distributes work accordingly, evaluates performance, and provides feedback

Interpersonal Skills: Works with others

   A. Participates as a Member of a Team – contributes to a group effort
   B. Teaches Others New Skills
   C. Serves Clients/Customers – works to satisfy customer's expectations
   D. Exercises Leadership – communicates ideas to justify position, persuades and convinces others, initiates responsible challenges to existing procedures and policies
   E. Negotiates – works toward agreements involving exchanges of resources, resolves divergent interests
   F. Works with Diversity – works well with men and women from different backgrounds

Information: Acquires and uses information.

   A. Acquires and Evaluates Information
   B. Organizes and Maintains Information

C. Interprets and Communicates Information

D. Uses Computers to Process Information

Systems: Understands complex inter-relationships

A. Understands Systems – knows how social, organizational, and technical systems work, and operates effectively with them

B. Monitors and Corrects Performance – distinguishes trends, predicts impact on operations

C. Improves or Designs Systems – suggests modifications to existing systems and develops new or alternative systems to improve performance

Technology: Works with a variety of technologies

A. Selects Technology – chooses procedures, tools, or equipment including computers and related technologies

B. Applies Technology to Task – understands overall intent and proper procedures for setup and operation of equipment

C. Maintains and Troubleshoots Equipment

A THREE-PART FOUNDATION

Basic Skills: Reads, writes, and performs arithmetic and mathematical operations; listens and speaks

A. Reading – locates, understands, and interprets written information in prose and documents such as newspapers, textbooks, computerized information

B. Writing – communicates thoughts, ideas, information, and messages in writing, and creates letters, reports and sales messages

C. Arithmetic/Mathematics – performs basic computations and approaches practical problems by choosing appropriately from a variety of mathematical techniques

D. Listening – receives, attends to, interprets, and responds to verbal messages and other cues

E. Speaking – organizes ideas and communicates orally

Thinking Skills: Thinks creatively, makes decisions, solves problems, visualizes, knows how to learn and reason

A. Creative Thinking – generates new ideas

B. Decision Making – specifies goals and constraints, generates alternatives, considers risks, and evaluates and selects the best alternative

C. Problem Solving – recognizes problems and devises and implementation of a plan of action

D. Seeing Things in the Mind's Eye – organizes and processes symbols, pictures, objects, and other information

E. Knowing How to Learn – uses efficient learning techniques to acquire and apply new skills and knowledge

F. Reasoning – discovers a rule or principle underlying the relationship between two or more objects and applies it when solving a problem

Personal Qualities: Displays responsibility, self-esteem, sociability, self-management, integrity, and honesty

A. Responsibility – exerts a high level of effort and preserves toward goal attainment
B. Self-Esteem – believes in own self-worth and maintains a positive view of self
C. Sociability – demonstrates understanding, friendliness, empathy, and politeness in group settings
D. Self-Management – assesses self accurately, sets personal goals, monitors progress, and exhibits self control
E. Integrity/Honesty – chooses ethical courses of action

UNIT ONE
THE BUSINESS OF DESIGN

CHAPTER 1: THE APPAREL MANUFACTURER

SUPPLEMENTAL TEACHING INFORMATION

Begin the lecture by diagramming the organization of a typical manufacturer as follows:

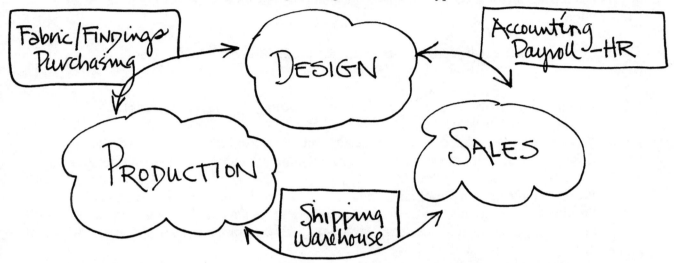

The text explains the three primary departments in a manufacturing firm. Back-up departments perform functions that allow the flow of product to continue unhampered and augment the three main departments. In small companies, one person may perform one or more of these jobs. Communication among all the people responsible for developing and producing product is critical. Computerized companies utilize systems to track myriad details, such as prices, resources, specifications, and other important information needed to produce a garment. Constant communication among all persons involved in the process requires workers to understand the entire manufacturing flow. Computer links to contractors or the production floor bring designers into the decision-making loop to resolve problems.

It is important to emphasize to your students that the major departments in an apparel company (manufacturing + sales + design/product development) are a circle with each major department constantly interacting with the others.

For example, designers often write sales manuals. They often participate in sales meetings to inform the sales staff how to sell the line. The designer frames the merchandise in the context of seasonal trends, colors, silhouettes, and details. Salespeople use this information to create their sales pitch and formulas to sell multiple units of coordinated sportswear lines or to push the best bodies in item and dress lines.

1

The design department usually creates a style sheet to assist the sales staff in identifying styles, prices and the assortment offered. Designers may even follow their products into retail stores to work with customers, though this is mostly typical of higher-priced merchandise.

Sales people should provide the designer and merchandiser with constant feedback from both retail buyers and actual customers once the merchandise has been shipped. This could include special requests for styles and colors that are missing in the line. Retail buyers often describe or give salespeople a garment that is selling well to incorporate into a future line.

The design department also works closely with the production department in several ways:

1. Provides information about trims, fabrics, interlining, thread color, and other components of each garment.
2. Works with the production pattern maker and production manager on production fittings to make sure the style of the garment is maintained when a standard size is made from the sample garment.
3. Prepares a resource list including the price of all components in the garment. Production management software like Gerber's WebPDM begins collecting data in the design room and is used to keep track of all the components of the garment throughout the production process.
4. The designer should track what is selling and record the results for future reference. Good merchandising involves repeating styles, colors, and trends that sell well. The designer must know which items are "hot" in order to create versions of them for the next line.

The production department relates to design because it is responsible for producing stock garments in a practical way using the most economical techniques to duplicate the samples created in the design room. The production manager usually communicates daily with the designer while the line is prepared for production to clarify small details that can make the cutting and sewing process less costly.

Email skills are critical for all personnel in product development and production. Designers and production staff must have the ability to clearly describe and write about all aspects of the production cycle. This is true of product that is manufactured domestically or abroad.

Slide Show of a Manufacturing Plant

A slide or Power Point show visually describing each step of the manufacturing process is an excellent learning tool. Use the diagram, *The Major Steps in Manufacturing a Garment,* on page 39 as a "shooting script" to create your own slide show. Digital images may be integrated quickly into a Power Point presentation. Take several photographs of each operation from various angles. Feature a long shot, as well as a close-up of machines in operation so students can relate to the job being done. Arrange the slides as soon as possible so you will remember the nuances of what you photographed.

Use photos outside the factory and in the garment district to orient your students. Inexpensive titles can be created by writing on cement with chalk, taking photographs of street and other commercial signs and preparing large, hand lettered sheets and photographing them. Prepare a script with commentary to accompany the slides.

A slide show should lead into a detailed discussion of the diagram of *The Major Steps in Manufacturing a Garment*. Emphasize the process steps that are influenced or actually done using a computer. Depending on the sophistication of the factory photographed, some of the processes that could be computerized may still be done manually. The industry as of 2003 is in the process of converting to CAD/CAM systems and there are still companies that have not integrated computers into their processes.

Invite guest speakers who are specialists in one aspect of apparel production. Encourage them to elaborate on the details of their job. Ask them to discuss the problem solving aspects of their daily tasks.

The instructor's challenge for the next five years (2003-2008) is to inform students of the technology available to facilitate each phase of the product development, pre-production, construction, and distribution processes, and to prepare them to perform the function both manually and utilizing a computer system.

Computer Assisted Apparel Production

Computerization of apparel production process began in the early 1970s. Camsco was a pioneer in the field. They developed a system that automated grading and marker making. The company was sold in the early 1980s to Gerber Garment Technology. "Gerber" dominated the domestic CAD market for sewn products for the next decade. Early systems cost $250,000, so only the largest companies could afford to purchase them. Competition from Micro Dynamics and Lectra (a French CAD/CAM system) began in the eighties as well. European technology was stimulated because early grading and marking technology was very similar to programs used to manufacture aircraft and missiles. Smaller companies like PAD and Scan Vec, as well as the emergence of companies that produced customized systems, expanded technology and resources rapidly. Prices became more affordable.

Early systems continued to concentrate on grading and marker making, and gradually graphic capability allowed companies to add textile design, art and design programs and finally pattern making software. Niche companies like BGA/SnapFashun developed specific types of programs dedicated to garment and textile design.

3

As systems became more affordable, fashion schools and colleges could afford to purchase CAD/CAM computers, and greater numbers could be trained to transfer their "table skills" to the new computer environment. Mirroring developments in the computer industry, increased memory made PC-based software possible. Gradually, PC technology replaced the huge stand-alone systems typical of the 1970-80s. Classrooms could now have multiple workstations to accommodate larger numbers of students.

Computer driven cutting machines increased demand for CAM software that prepared markers critical to the automated cutting process. Software that tracked production details expanded and computers eased managing myriad details associated with off-site production. Computers are now commonplace on the factory floor, tracking garments as they are manufactured, translating specifications, and calculating worker productivity and payments. Email connects all players in the production cycle and eliminates many communications glitches. Computers have facilitated integrating contractors, both domestic and foreign, into the production cycle.

The design room has been the last department to be automated. Reasons for this are described in the section entitled *What Will the Design Department of the Future Look Like?* Evaluation of the state of the industry in 2003 indicates that many companies are in the process of acquiring CAD/CAM systems. Recent fashion school graduates often value computer training more than the average apparel manufacturer. Tuka Tech, distributor of Scan Vec software, recently experimented with a "technology rental" outlet similar to Kinkos. People paid for time on a computer to access CAD/CAM software. Training is available for those unfamiliar with the TukaCAD system.

Size is no longer the deciding factor in determining which manufacturer will embrace high technology. In fact, savvy computer experts can start a small business using computer technology, talent, and a CAD/Cam system. The deciding factor seems to be developing a comfort level with technology and thoughtful integration of CAD/CAM systems into the product development and manufacturing process.

Industry Trends

During the late 1980s and continuing into the1990s, a significant shift in the fashion industry occurred. Although the east coast, New York specifically, maintained dominance as the center of American high fashion, the west coast surged ahead in the total volume of apparel produced. Southern California and Los Angeles, specializing in moderate and budget junior and women's wear, active sportswear, and surf wear, produced approximately 70% of the state's apparel and a smaller northern California industry centered in San Francisco produced the balance.

The surge in west coast apparel production diminished during the 2000s. The Los Angeles County Workforce Preparation and Economic Development Collaborative was commissioned to study the factors involved in the expansion of the industry on the west coast. The findings are significant for the industry nationwide. Project Director, Linda Wong of the Community Development Technology Center, wrote *Fashion Forward: Assessing the Future of Apparel Manufacturing in Los Angeles County* in 2002. The following reprint describes industry trends that affect apparel producers nationally and provides a wealth of information for fashion instructors. Copies of the complete report can be downloaded from the CD Tech website: http://.cdtech.org/workforce.

Labor Issues

Explore the labor issues surrounding the apparel industry in your locale. Ask students to research and respond to the following issues. Support from industry experts is helpful to understand these evolving and sometimes emotional issues:

1. Monitoring sewing contractors for compliance with federal and state Department of Labor regulations.
2. The history of organized labor in the United States.
3. The evolution of unions in specific cities and how they affected apparel production in that locale.
4. The relationship of retailers to the price paid to sewing contractors to construct a specific garment.
5. Analyze the cost of sewing a garment with the total wholesale cost of the item. Compare the final price with the cost of material, product development, sales, and profit.

The cost of labor in various areas of the United States must be compared to the cost of the labor in foreign countries. Factor in other costs like duty, customs, shipping, import brokers, bribes, inspection, oversight, and so forth as components of the cost of the garment.

GENERAL FASHION PROBLEMS

Research a Manufacturing Firm

Research a major garment manufacturer and draw up a profile of the divisions of the firm and the target customers. The best way to do this is to look at the entire product line, which is usually carried in an outlet or company owned store. Analyze the product by investigating the following:

Price line	Type of merchandise
Category of each division	Volume
Production methods	Publicly held company?
Target customers	Type of retail outlets
Promotion and advertising	

5

Look for information in trade newspapers and business magazines. Seek out promotional material, investor information, and annual reports for publicly held companies (stock available for public purchase), interview employees, and make personal observations.

Care Labels

Investigate the purpose of care instructions included in each garment. What necessary information must be included on the care label? Compare and contrast the use of the garment with its care instructions. For example, a silk blouse requires dry cleaning and this factor limits the use of the garment somewhat. Identify the RN number (a registration number issued to a manufacturer that must be printed on each garment produced to identify its origin.)

Garment Labels and Logos

Collect a variety of garment labels and company logos. Compare and contrast them to the merchandise they represent. Collect examples of woven and printed labels. Discuss the cost of labeling each garment. Are labels and manufacturers' names important to the sale of each garment? Identify labels used by retailers for their own product lines.

Computers Available to Assist Apparel Production/Design

Research the variety of computer assisted apparel products available in the market place. Resources include trade journals, observing demonstrations at trade shows or vendors, visiting sales offices and apparel companies who have computerized their production and design departments. Evaluate two similar programs using price, power, availability of training, service policy, and features to determine the best value for a small apparel manufacturing company.

MERCHANDISING PROBLEMS

Merchandise Presentation

Investigate a specific category of merchandising by visiting and studying a department in a large store or a specialty store. Discover and analyze the following things about the merchandising mix:
1. major vendors
2. price lines (sometimes called price zones) – the range from high to low and the most frequently used price ranges
3. vendors that sell fashion garments
4. the "bread and butter" or staples of the department/store
5. categories of apparel offered
6. size range
7. construction standards of specific price/categories
8. assortment – selection of sizes, colors, and styles (SKU = stock keeping units)

When you have complied the specifics of the merchandise offered by the store, contrast the merchandise mix to the store decor:

1. discuss the interior design of the store
2. what display techniques are used?
3. is music used to add to the atmosphere of the retail setting?
4. is the lighting effective?
5. is the merchandise arranged so it is attractive and easy to locate?
6. are dressing rooms convenient to the selling floor?
7. does the total store décor enhance the merchandise?
8. is it easy to find sizes on your own or does a sales person have to assist?

Take all these specific observations about the merchandise and how it was presented and use them to critique the store. How would you improve the store and make it more appealing to the target customer.

BEGINNING DESIGN PROBLEM

Diagnose Student Design Skills

Ask your students to design a garment that would typically be worn by a customer that approximates the age and life-style of the majority of your students. Select a specific season and category of apparel. This eliminates the research element, a topic discussed in later chapters. Test how well your students follow directions by making the assignment very specific. Require a sketch of a dress, top, pants, or coordinated sportswear outfit. Assign a specific fabric and the size of the sketch, number of figures on the page, media to be used and so forth. Use this as a way to diagnose the ability level of your students. Save to compare with later assignments as they become more proficient at sketching and design.

VOCABULARY

Refer to the *Word Finders* at the end of the chapter to devise a crossword puzzle to test the reading assignment you have given your students.

Acronyms

Every industry has a cluster of acronyms that are typical "alphabet soup" that allow people to shortcut their dialogue about technical issues. Start a list of these and encourage your students to use them in class discussions

CAD   Computer Aided Design
CAM   Computer Aided Manufacturing
CAN   California Apparel News

DOL	Department of Labor (both the federal and state levels)
DOS	Data Operating Systems (typical of older IBM computers)
EDI	Electronic Data Interchange
Email	Electronic mail
GGT	Gerber Garment Technology
HP	Hewlett Packard (computers used by Lectra, GGT)
IBM	International Business Machines ("Big Blue" computer manufacturer)
ILGWU	International Ladies Garment Workers Union (now UNITE)
PC	Personal Computer (uses PC based software instead of MAC software)
PDM	Product Data Management software
PDS	Pattern Design System (Gerber software)
PFP	Prepared For Print (textiles ready to accept a print)
POS	Point of Sale
SAM	Standard Allowed Minutes (used to calculate sewing costs)
SKU	Stock Keeping Units
[TC]2	Textile Clothing Technology Corporation (TC-square)
UGWA	United Garment Workers of America
UNITE	Union of Needletrades, Industrial & Textile Employees
UPS	Unit Production System (Eton system for delivering garment pieces to sewers)
WWD	Women's Wear Daily
WWW	World Wide Web

TEST AND QUIZ QUESTIONS

1. Discuss the advantages and disadvantages of an inside versus an outside shop. (pages 9-11)

2. List the major departments in an apparel firm. (page 5)

3. Define contracting and list three typical phases of production that can be contracted out.   (pages 8-11)

4. What is a spec sheet used for? (pages 13-14)

5. Defined balanced sourcing.   (page 13)

6. Describe the relationship between minimum wage and piecework. (pages 26-27)

7. Describe the tasks of a production patternmaker. (pages 17-18)

8. Define the term *grading* and describe how computers have changed the tasks of a grader. (pages 18-20)

9. What is a marker? (page 21)

10. Describe at least three types of bundling systems typically used in apparel production. (pages 23-24)

11. What are *Federal Stitch Types*, and how is the designation used in an apparel factory. (pages 29-30)

12. Explain the role of a time and motion analysis of the sewing process. (pages 25-26 and 30-31)

13. Explain the interaction between a designer and sales personnel. (page 53)

14. Discuss three important innovations that will dramatically change the way garments are designed and delivered to the ultimate customer. (pages 49-52)

15. Do you think mass customization will alter the existing method of shopping for apparel? (pages 46-47)

16. Compare and contrast the role and responsibilities of a freelance designer with an in-house designer. (pages 53-54)

CHAPTER 2: WHAT DOES A DESIGNER DO?

SUPPLEMENTARY TEACHING INFORMATION

Most students do not understand that a designer is really a product development engineer. The novice imagines a person in an ideal environment, sketching glamorous clothes (never a budget blouse!), selecting from an infinite variety of beautiful fabrics with little thought of how much they cost, and creating a garment that they would personally love to wear. This is not reality. Chapter 2 presents the great variety of experiences a designer can have—along with a smattering of the responsibilities and preparation involved in creating a commercial line. The instructor should reinforce the reality by emphasizing and, better yet, demonstrating some of the skills a designer must have to be successful.

Focus on the wide range of other jobs available in the industry that are related to product development. Many of your students will realize that they are not cut out to be designers because they lack talent or tenacity to be both creative and a businessperson, but they may have the ability to become an excellent patternmaker or successful design support person.

If your students have not taken a class in sewing, draping, sketching, or pattern making, demonstrate these skills to them. Drape a basic bodice or skirt on a dress form in muslin. Use only half a drape and explain why this method is used. This demonstration should not be very technical. The purpose is to acquaint the beginner with a method for making two-dimensional fabric into a three-dimensional shape. Stress the flexibility of draping. Identify the darts, point of bust, arm's eye, and other important components of the dress form as you drape. Many students cannot visualize how a three-dimensional shape can be returned to a two-dimensional pattern. Spread your drape out, true it up, and quickly make a flat pattern explaining that this information is critical to the fit and design of a garment.

Drape a bodice using a knit fabric and explain why there is no need for darts and gores. Explain the stretch factor common to knits and the construction differences between a knit fabric and a woven. Discuss how a knit garment is finished and compare it to the facings, collars, and structural elements possible when designing a woven garment.

Show your class a manufacturer's pattern and explain commercial seam allowances, notches, markings, and how the pattern sews together. Explain "walking" two pattern pieces (matching the edges to make sure they will sew together accurately.) Stack several sizes of a bodice, skirt, sleeve and/or pant pattern into a nest to show how a pattern grows according to specific proportions when graded.

Discuss:
1. how a commercial pattern differs from a home sewing pattern
2. how essential the universal language of notches and seam allowances is to the manufacturing process
3. how computer created patterns compare to manually produced patterns and how fit is important to both
4. discuss a pattern chart and its purposes
5. show the tools typically used by a manual pattern maker and what each is used for

Demonstrate flat pattern work by showing your class how to shift darts in the basic front bodice. Compare the different methods and results achieved by draping, pattern manipulation, and computer produced patterns.

Compare and contrast a working sketch (croquis) with several illustrations. Compare a newspaper apparel ad for an expensive garment with a trade paper editorial sketch. Discuss the purpose of each and why they differ. Explain that it would be very difficult to make a pattern from a high-style illustration, but the garment is glamorized to appeal to the customer.

Many instructors integrate *Inside Fashion Design* into courses in pattern making, using the text as outside reading to orient students to the business aspects of designing and concentrating on pattern making exercises in the classroom. The comprehensive pattern making book written by Helen Armstrong entitled *Patternmaking for Fashion Design, 4th Edition,* also published by Prentice Hall is the perfect companion text.

It is critical for students to understand that the technical skills (pattern making, draping, textile selection and testing, and understanding construction techniques) is just as critical for a designer as are creativity, a business sense, and good taste level.

FIELD TRIP RECOMMENDATIONS

Visit a designer or invite one to speak to your class. If you have no manufacturers in your area, watch newspapers for visiting designers who may be promoting their lines at local stores. Either attend the trunk show or contact the retailer to see if the designer is available to speak to your class.

Appropriate topics for the guest speaker are:

1. specific responsibilities of this designer
2. methods (s)he uses to formulate ideas
3. production methods for the first sample (CAD, draping, etc.)
4. description of a typical day
5. comment on current fashion and textile trends
6. background and personal career evolution
7. important parts of a designer's education

11

If possible, visit a design room. Ask if the assistants and other staff members can explain their jobs and how they were trained for their positions. Your students will relate to young people who have just started their jobs as well as the well-established veterans.

Visit or invite a buyer from a local retail store to speak to your class. Ask them to discuss the following topics:
- vendors and the wide range of apparel available for their customers
- price points so your students begin to differentiate between economic markets
- innovative apparel lines designed by young designers
- evaluation of their products and their place in the market
- description of a buying trip to New York, a regional market, and a visit from a road sales person representing a specific line
- the role of a buying office

GENERAL FASHION PROBLEMS

Retail Store Research
Assign a research trip to a local department store. If a buyer or department manager is available, have him/her discuss the specific department. This assignment is also an excellent field trip for your entire class.

Evaluate the hanger appeal of garments and discuss how a garment has to pass this critical test to sell well. Discuss garments (bodies) that are currently selling well. Identify the major vendors in the department, their price range, and the kind of merchandise they are known for. Look for the staples and the fashion-forward merchandise and discuss how they often appeal to the same customer.

Ask the students to evaluate the environment and layout of the store or department and discuss the relationship of the merchandise to its presentation. Explain that new merchandise is usually grouped at the front of the store to take advantage of its novelty. Store managers routinely rearrange the selling floor, moving older merchandise toward the back of the department and featuring the latest deliveries. Ask your students to compare and contrast the presentation of similar merchandise (example, sportswear) in two different categories (junior versus missy, active versus spectator).

Trunk Shows
Send your students to a trunk show or informal fashion show and ask them to interview the designer or sales representative presenting the merchandise. You can also view a virtual fashion show on the Internet and ask for a similar evaluation. Some important questions are:

1. who is the customer?
2. what is the price range and merchandise category?
3. does the customer buy the apparel at full price or is a reduced price more important?

4. does the customer make multiple purchases?
5. what fashion trends are reflected in the current line?

Another excellent experience is attending a home-based sales party where a community member shows an apparel line to a group of customers and takes orders for future purchases. You may also use catalogs featuring coordinated sportswear and dresses to provide an example for student analysis of a product line.

Market Survey

Assign your students to survey the market. Review the categories listed on pages 82-83 and ask your students to use retail stores, newspaper advertisements, catalogs, and fashion magazines. List vendors in all the categories, designating their approximate price range and typical customer:

Example:

Daytime dresses:	Liz Claiborne	Moderate	Conservative customer
Evening dresses:	Tadashi	Better	Contemporary customer
Coordinated SW:	Ellen Tracy	Bridge	Upscale career

Stress the tremendous variety of apparel available to the public at many price ranges and through a wide variety of retailers. These manufacturers provide career resources for fashion students.

Job Seeking

Have each student write a résumé and cover letter to the company of their choice. Research the various styles of résumés first. Many inexpensive paperback books are available that provide strategies and examples of résumés and cover letters for many industries. Ask each person to submit a preliminary draft of their rèsumè and discuss how to phrase experience and educational entries in the most positive way. Distribute typical employment applications and have students fill them out to match their résumé stressing neatness and legibility.

Mock interviews among students and their peers are positive exercises for developing confidence in a stressful situation. Ask students to role-play as the human resources interviewer and job seeker. Consider using video playbacks and industry professionals to make the interview sessions reflective of the real world.

Require advanced design students to present their résumé and portfolio to a committee of industry professionals. Prepare a rating sheet so each guest can evaluate the student's presentation. Discuss the results with each candidate after the interview. Follow up by interviewing the student again and stressing how they have improved and what the next steps are to be completely convincing as a job applicant.

MERCHANDISING PROBLEMS

Lessons from the Mark Down Rack

Evaluate a mark down rack. Why was the merchandise marked down? Consider the following possibilities:

Unattractive	Odd lots, few sizes	Fits poorly
Bad color	Priced too high	Damaged
Unseasonable	Styling is too radical	

Explain special purchases—those garments purchased at a lower price than regular stock, brought in at full price for a short time and then marked down to a reasonable mark up (called *cancellation of mark up)*. Often, this merchandise has been commissioned from a vendor and copied from a more expensive garment. Ask students to identify and evaluate these garments. Does the lower price compensate for the fact they are sold later in the season and often made in less desirable fabrics than the original style?

BEGINNING CREATIVE PROBLEMS

Accessory Design

Ask your students to design a basic dress, coordinated outfit, or suit. Design accessories to work with this basic garment to change the look. Take a basic garment and modify it and the accessories so different customers would purchase the ensemble. Use store ads, catalogs, or magazines for research.

Dress a Fictional Character

Select a group of characters from novels, plays, movies, or a television series. Assign each student a different female character. Design a daytime wardrobe for this "personality/customer" as well as an evening ensemble that fits the situation in which the character is set. Select appropriate fabric and design the garments.

ADVANCED CREATIVE PROBLEM

Design Apparel Based on Interior Life Styles

Clip a group of interiors from shelter magazines (*House Beautiful, Martha Steward's Living, Country Living, Traditional Home, Elle Décor, Architectural Digest, Veranda,* and so forth.) Choose distinctive rooms photographed on full pages.

Ask each student to envision the customer who would live in the home and design a garment that would be appropriate to wear in the room. Develop a personal profile of the person that includes occupation, color and style preferences, and taste level. Sketch the garment and personality on opaque paper and cut the figure out. Mount the interior photo on a board and glue the figure illustration over the photograph.

VOCABULARY

Begin introducing fashion vocabulary by requiring students to read trade newspapers and select current "hot phrases" and terms used to describe garments and colors. Emphasize these will change from year to year.

Ask the students to name merchandise groups. Designers often have to name either groups or individual bodies. Examples I have used include:

Heather and Leather	Country Cloth
Denim and Diamonds	Vintage Visions

Have fun with this!

Acronyms

CEO	Chief Executive Officer
CFO	Chief Financial Officer
COO	Chief Operating Officer
IT	Information Technology
DM	Divisional Merchandiser
RTW	Ready To Wear

TEST AND QUIZ QUESTIONS

1. Describe how a hot body is used in later seasons to continue good sales. (page 59)

2. How will computer change the way a customer can purchase apparel? (pages 61-62)

3. Analyze the first things that appeal to a customer. How do most people relate vision with the tactile sense when evaluating clothes? (pages 63-64)

4. How should the care and durability of a garment relate to its design? (pages 66-67)

5. Describe the differences between a working sketch and a fashion illustration. (pages 67-68)

6. Describe three workers typically found in the design room besides a designer. (pages 70-72)

7. What is merchandising a line? (pages 72-74)

8. Compare and contrast a sample with a garment that has been reengineered by the production pattern maker. (pages 75-77)

9. What is EDI and what type of merchandise is it most often used with? (page 77)

10. Describe three methods of advertising and promoting apparel to the ultimate customer. (pages 77-79)

11. What is a taste level? Why is it important? (page 82)

12. Compare and contrast junior, bridge, designer, and missy apparel categories. (pages 82-84)

13. How do the portfolio and résumé fit into a job interview? (pages 84-86)

CHAPTER 3: SOURCES OF INSPIRATION

SUPPLEMENTARY TEACHING INFORMATION

Resource Material

Collect a full range of foreign and domestic fashion publications and resources. These change constantly. Evaluate each report, magazine, web site, and source. Discuss which sources are most appropriate for each category of merchandise. For example, a children's wear designer would look at *Seventeen* to see what young teens are wearing and would also research magazines that feature children's apparel. Be sure to show your students the upscale foreign fashion magazines even though they are costly.

Differentiate between magazines and other resources that provide second-hand fashion information (magazines, fashion reports, newspapers) and reference material that stimulates an idea (color reports, innovative street fashions, original high fashion, and couture shows) that is then translated into an apparel trend.

Indirect inspiration also includes museum exhibits, textile designs, fine arts, and other cultural and trend information from related fields—but not direct information for fashion reporting services or media.

The Fashion Cycle Chart

Tracing a real fashion cycle is an excellent way to demonstrate many aspects of timing. It is important for a designer to recognize where the customer is on the fashion cycle. The amount of innovative, fashion-forward styling a customer will purchase is dependent on the apparel category, price range, locale (urban or rural), domestic or European, and so forth.

Prepare a visual chart of a current fashion cycle starting with:

1. coverage of a new fashion trend in an upscale publication or on a designer web site
2. search for an interpretation of the trend in American fashion journals emphasizing changes made to the original design concept that make it more salable to the fashion forward customer
3. collect versions and knock offs of the garment….see if it is being copied in European markets too
4. identify interpretations of the trend by American high fashion designers

At the next stage, many domestic designers of moderately priced conservative apparel modify the original silhouette and interpret it for their more conservative customers. This process is accelerated by the instant access domestic designers have to European and Japanese collections via the Internet.

5. collect photos of knock offs and versions made by the domestic moderate market and trace through popular women's magazines like *Glamour, Cosmopolitan, In Style, Mademoiselle,* and *Elle*...note the price ranges
6. trace the style to the popular fashion catalogs and finally to promotional vendors and mark down racks

Paste up these articles, photographs and other examples on a board that illustrates the fashion cycle. Include dates of each phase of the cycle and identify how quickly the style lasted.

The Season/Retail Cycle

Discuss store timing. Refer to the chart on pages 97 and 98. Develop a questionnaire based on some or all of the following questions. Distribute them to sample group and ask for some personal details like gender, age, occupation, and income level. Analyze the results and discussion them with your students, relating the response to potential customers:

1. Do you purchase clothes when the selection is the greatest (often two months prior to being able to wear them) or when the weather dictates a new wardrobe?
2. How many purchases are impulse driven, selected to wear immediately?
3. How important is buying a bargain compared to the style or quality of a garment?
4. Are you willing to drive long distances to an outlet center to purchase a value item, or is time and convenience more important to you?
5. Do you like to shop? Would you prefer to purchase clothing through the mail from a catalog?
6. Have you ever gone to a home shopping party where a hostess presented the apparel and worked with each client to select garments for later delivery? Did you like the experience?
7. Is it more important to have exactly the right garment than to purchase it and wear it immediately?
8. If you were traveling to a warm resort in December, could you buy a bathing suit at your favorite store? (If you live in the sun belt, substitute purchasing ski clothes for a bathing suit.)
9. What percent of your wardrobe is "fashion forward" and what percent is basics?
10. Where do you purchase your apparel:
    A full service department store
    Specialty store
    An outlet or vintage/second hand store
    Catalog or mail order
    Internet
    TV shopping network

Sketch Book

Teach your students how to draw quick sketches using the tracing method and a basic figure croquis and require them to start a sketchbook. Build their skills in this necessary activity. Demonstrate how to sketch half a garment in a few seconds.

Allow the students five minutes to sketch a moderately complicated hanging garment. Check the details and proportions and have them correct their sketches. Display a second garment for one minute. Have each student study the garment without making a sketch. Hide the garment and give them two minutes to draw as much of it as they can remember. Continue to provide them with examples---sometimes just details, sometimes entire garments---and push them to sketch faster and with greater accuracy as their skills develop. These exercises prepare them to sketch during the slide shows, as they shop retail stores and people on the streets. Write notes beside the sketch to describe trims and fabric.

Fashion Reports

Fashion reports are an important aid for apparel designers. Collect examples of reports for research in your class. If you are unable to purchase them, ask for donations from publishers, designers, and retailers. It is not critical that the copies be current. Demonstrate, either by sketching yourself or selecting photographs of designs that are versions of those shown in a design report, how domestic manufacturers interpret high fashion designers.

FIELD TRIP RECOMMENDATIONS

Visiting a retail store is very informative after reading Chapter 3. The exercises in the first two chapters introduce the student to merchandise as a product suitable for other people instead of clothes for themselves. Assign a systematic visit to a retailer using the shopping worksheets on pages 130-131.

VISUALS

Slide shows of the Paris couture and *prêt-à-porter* shows are given in most fashion markets by the Fashion Group, retailers, or reporting services. Urge these organizations to allow students to attend these shows. Often dated slide reports and the accompanying script are donated to fashion schools. Use them to describe how to sketch and analyze the trends that are presented.

The Fashion Group International (FGI) is a non-profit group for fashion professionals, based in New York with regional branches around the world. Membership was originally limited to women but now includes men and women. A mission of the group is to encourage people to enter the industry, and scholarships, career days, and student memberships are available. Students are often invited to events at minimal cost. Fashion instructors are welcome as members. Two current members sponsor a prospective new member and dues are reasonable. The web address is: www.fgi.org

Inquire with the parent group for information on regional branches:

The Fashion Group International
597 Fifth Avenue, 8th floor
New York, New York 10017
212-593-1715

GENERAL FASHION PROBLEMS

Shopping retail stores has been a consistent theme throughout this instructor's manual because:

1. retail clothing stores and catalogs are available in most areas of the United States
2. the end product of design and manufacturing can be analyzed first hand and the success or failure of an item determined by its status on the selling floor
3. students must get into the habit of constantly shopping retail stores because all fashion professionals analyze the merit and success of a product in a retail setting.

Retail apparel stores in New York are traditionally open late Monday evenings and usually visiting fabric sales people, designers, manufacturers, and other industry professionals cruise the aisles analyzing fashion trends before heading for dinner and their hotel rooms.

Guide your students so they develop a heightened awareness of the product when they are shopping. Instructors should also shop stores whenever possible with their students to encourage them to develop good work habits and to facilitate their access to high priced departments where students may feel uncomfortable.

Encourage your students to develop objectivity when analyzing apparel but not to loose their consumer instincts and common sense. Ask them to respond to what they see analytically. Ask for specifics---sketches, written reports, photographs, and oral reports are all important.

MERCHANDISING PROBLEMS

Identify a trend across several markets or the evolution of an item in one market. Use multiple resources to report on the trend including stores, catalogs, magazines, and so forth. Identify current items and general trends in color, fabrication, and styling. Refer to the diagram of the fashion cycle and have students replicate this with a different format or item to track.

BEGINNING DESIGN PROBLEMS

Research

Plan a field trip to a museum to view period clothing. Try to isolate a specific period or designer so your students can concentrate their research on the period or kind of apparel before visiting the display. Ask them to sketch a garment and style details and start a collection of ideas based on the exhibit. Discuss the general proportion and style themes used to style the clothes. Have the students design one or more contemporary garments using inspiration from the exhibit and their research.

Event Inspiration

Analyze the sources of inspiration listed in the chapter. Make a resource list of potential field trips for your locale. Follow current events and suggest your students attend interesting events as inspiration. These can be as diverse as attending a rodeo to study western apparel or an art gallery opening to catch the urban avante guarde crowd. Require students to make preliminary sketches at the event and select one idea from several they have collected. Design a garment or ensemble appropriate for a person to wear to the specific event.

ADVANCED CREATIVE DESIGN PROBLEMS

Many of these problems make excellent final projects now that students have enough basic information on design and production processes to tackle a long-range problem with a number of specific requirements.

Life Style Problem

(Adapt this problem for merchandising students by requiring them to clip photographs and present them as a collage or report instead of sketching the garments.)

Analyze various customers and design specific products that have been defined by price point and season. The life style, age, and income level of each category should dictate styling. Have students select their customer randomly by drawing "from a hat"…no favorites here!

21

Each student should create a profile of the customer they have selected including the following characteristics: age, size, income level, urban/rural dweller, vacation, job, activities during the day and evening, sports, cars, cosmetics/perfumes used, and so forth.

Once the profile has been established, answer these questions:

1. what stores would this person shop in?
2. where are their clothes on the fashion cycle?
3. what fabrics would they wear?
4. how would they take care of their clothes?
5. how much would they spend on apparel items?

Design a small group of garments (ten to fifteen) that will carry your customer through a week of typical activities. The instructors and student designer should agree on a typical price range for the apparel. Other components of the design project should be specified. Consider:

1. select appropriate fabric styles
2. select colors for a specific season
3. sketch preliminary items, review with instructor and revise ideas
4. design or select appropriate garments
5. mount on a board with fabrics and trim details
6. write a description of the client, life style findings, etc.
7. present your project to the entire class

Category suggestions:

Big and Beautiful – the plus size woman
Young, Married, and Making It – affluent young urbanite
Domestic Goddess – the rural or suburban housewife
Auntie Mame – the older flamboyant woman
Swinging Career Single – the unattached contemporary worker
College Cutie – college co-ed
Free Spirited Single – resort or beach dweller
Budget-Conscious Business Woman – budget looks, OK for business
Teen Queen – the young junior with both school and a job
Volunteer Matron – the socially active 40+ woman
Gertie the Gardener – the retired homebody
Success at All Costs – upwardly mobile young executive
The Sales Sultan – salesman/woman of _____ product
Toddler Teacher – a grammar school teacher

Make additions that are related to your community. This project can also be made into a very exciting visual presentation. Take slides of the exceptional projects and use them to introduce the student work to professionals or other students.

The visualization process of this project is very important and emphasizes the SCANS skills of *seeing a finished project in the mind's eye.* Other important skills taught by this project include *understanding social systems, solving problems,* and *organizing ideas and communicating them both orally and in writing.*

Cultural Inspiration

Collect photographs and illustrations of Asian costume. Oriental inspiration can also be tied in with a museum or craft exhibit. Textile patterns, costumes and typical colors of each nationality are important research assignments. Separate Japanese from that of China, Korea, and other Asian cultures, and focus on one.

If you select Japan, research ukiyo-e prints (literal translation is *pictures of the floating world.)* These traditional wood block prints are particularly inspirational because they depict actors, geisha, and people doing daily tasks. Many excellent reference books are available on this genre. Kimonos also have a rich textile history and unique colorations and patterns. Contemporary Japanese designers constantly return to their fine arts and folk cultures for inspiration, and these resources have inspired western costume for decades.

Using primary sources of inspiration, ask students to design garments using the shapes, colors, layers, and other details observed to create modern garments. Illustrate the ensembles in color and fabricate the designs and include swatches.

American Quilts

Research and study traditional American quilt patterns. Many exciting books are available on this subject. If you or your students have personal quilts, share them with the class. Explain the four main techniques used in making traditional quilts:

1. patching (geometric designs, crazy quilts)
2. quilting (filling and backing plain fabric)
3. appliqué (Hawaiian quilts)
4. surface embroidery

Many reference and craft books explain these techniques in detail.

Ask students to design a quilt pattern and color motif and execute it in a small patch or textile painting. Design a simple garment using the quilt fabric.

Vocabulary

Build student vocabulary by connecting the name of a designer with their product. Devise sight recognition by mounting styles typical of various designers on boards and have students identify the designer.

Play games with color names. Designers often have to name the colors offered in a group. Ask students to come up with as many different color names as possible for a range of colors: reds, blues, peach, greens, black, and white. Assign two students one color; have one student invent names typical of junior apparel and the other name those that would appeal to a mature customer. Have fun with this!

Acronyms

BGA	Bill Glazer Associates (publishers of Report West and SnapFashun)
CAN	California Apparel News
CNN	Cable News Network
DKNY	Donna Karen New York (Karen's sportswear line)
DNR	Daily News Record
GQ	Gentleman's Quarterly
MD	Mark Down
SA	Seventh Avenue
V and A	Victoria and Albert Museum in London
WWD	Women's Wear Daily
W	The consumer magazine version of WWD

TEST AND QUIZ QUESTIONS

1. Explain the term *fashion from the streets*. (pages 95 and 99-101)

2. Compare and contrast glossy fashion magazines with trade magazines and newspapers and name the most successful crossover publication in woman's wear. (pages 99 and 104-108)

3. Diagram and explain the fashion cycle. (pages 95-96)

4. Describe three trade magazines or papers and list the markets they serve. (page 104)

5. How do designers use fashion reports? Name at least three reports. (pages 111-115)

6. What is scrap and how is it used? (page118)

7.   Who initiates color predictions? (page 115)

8. Why is it important to research other designers' products; what would you look for?   (pages 108-110 and 119-120)

9. Describe how to use a sketch book.   (pages 99-101 and 118-119)

10. Describe two primary sources of inspiration and three secondary resources. (pages 126-129)

CHAPTER 4: DESIGNING A SUCCESSFUL GARMENT

SUPPLEMENTAL TEACHING INFORMATION

The material in this chapter should be illustrated by using a variety of clothing and accessories on many different figure types to demonstrate the principles and elements of design. As a bonus, students should learn how to dress themselves as well as others with problem figure types. Use examples from the late 20th century to define the design principles and avoid the temptation to only look at current fashions. Silhouettes and style details are constantly reinterpreted from the recent past and using contemporary examples may eliminate trends that can be gleaned from vintage apparel.

Real Garments

Begin collecting period and contemporary garments and accessories. Most prominent fashion schools realize the importance of a resource collection and solicit period clothing to use as student inspiration. A study collection is not as precious as a museum collection and some pieces must be displayed on a real figure or dress form to be truly appreciated. Garments can be used to teach students how to sketch and illustrate as well as demonstrate design principles.

Use real garments to compare and contrast construction methods of better, moderate, and budget garments. The quality of fit and construction has a great deal to do with the effectiveness of a garment. Turn the garment inside out and point out the variety of finishings, linings, and structure that give a garment form.

Divide your class into teams and have each group research a different principle or element and present good and bad examples to the class. Encourage them to look for examples in their own wardrobes if you do not have a collection of garments available.

Assemble a simple wardrobe of dark and light basic tops and bottoms and several bright accessories (like a red belt, bright scarves, colored panty hose, and so forth) to demonstrate many of the illusions discussed in the text. Dress a variety of figure types in these garments and have the class analyze the results.

Collect examples of bad design, both actual garments, and photographs. Present them to you class and ask them to identify the problems and analyze why some garment are unsuccessful.

Slides and Photographs of Garments

Though two-dimensional representations do not equal the real thing, slides are easy to store and can be quickly and efficiently presented. Digital images can be included in Power Point presentations that illustrate lectures on principles and design concepts.

Compare and analyze period clothing defining the silhouette and illusion that was popular during a specific era. Identify the style principles and exaggerations that were used to achieve the vintage look. Trace the trend to modern apparel.

GENERAL FASHION PROBLEMS

If you are a woman, analyze your figure. If you are a man, select a public figure or friend to work with---collecting a photograph for analysis if a person is not available. Women's Wear Daily, W, and other glossy magazines often do this exercise and you can collect articles to serve as references for your students.

Step 1...the analysis

1. define the figure type
2. list positives and negatives
3. determine the illusion you want to create to bring your figure closest to the current fashion ideal

Step 2...research

1. refer to the text for basic formulas to create the image you want and list them
2. sketch, clip examples from magazines/catalogs, or try on four or five outfits and analyze them in light of the formulas you have determined are most effective for your body type
3. eliminate the least flattering outfits

Step 3...move toward the fashion ideal

1. select garments that use the formula you have found to be most flattering
2. explore a variety of color solutions to find the most attractive colors and values for all parts of your body
3. add accessories that reinforce the design principle you have found to be most flattering

Summarize the analysis and research. Sketch, photograph, or illustrate garments that are most flattering for your figure type.

MERCHANDISING PROBLEM

Select a specialty apparel category based on size, like the plus-size woman, maternity wear, petites, or tall sizes. Send your students out to shop stores that cater to the selected figure type. Have each student provide a customer profile that includes the figure problem and the life style of the customer. Emphasize the creativity needed to respond to all problems, not just the aesthetic ones. Shop and least one department store and one specialty store that caters to the selected customer. Analyze the merchandise offered.

- Does the assortment reflect the needs of the customer?
- Do mannequins, models, and sales people relate to the customer?
- What are the limitations imposed on a customer who has a figure problem versus one who wears a standard size?

Answer these questions:

1. is there a good assortment (selection of sizes and styles)?
2. does the price seem to be a barrier to sales?
3. are there obvious gaps in the assortment?
4. do the displays relate well to the customer?
5. do sales people assist customers and reflect their figure problem so there is a comfort level between them?

If possible, encourage your students to ask sales people for their value judgments on the assortment. Which items are selling best? What general fashion trends are reflected in the stock? Is the merchandise more appealing than you imagined? What styling devices are used repeatedly to make the garments more appealing and closer to the fashion ideal?

BEGINNING DESIGN PROBLEMS

Assign a figure problem as a design project. Ask the students to research the problems inherent for the customer (using criteria from the Merchandising Problem.) For example:

Design a wardrobe of 15 to 20 interchangeable pieces that will be the maternity wardrobe for a mother-to-be who is 25 and lives in suburbia. She has a part-time office job that she will keep while pregnant. The garments should be designed for winter and spring (typically a six-month period when maternity clothes are worn.) The resulting ensembles should be appropriate for a wide range of events and be carefully planned so the price of the whole wardrobe is not excessive. Consult the chapter for style lines that slenderize, heighten and minimize the stomach. Shop maternity stores and evaluate the merchandise offered.

Consider the mentality of pregnancy. In many eras, women wanted to cover the bulge of their stomachs. In other times, women celebrate pregnancy and call attention to their coming motherhood. The social concepts of a period affect fashion and how women feel about their bodies.

Fabric selection is critical to the success of this interchangeable wardrobe. Remember that pregnant women are usually warmer than normal, so layers are critical for comfort as well as versatility. Plan items with a closely related color story. Include casual garments as well as street and evening clothes.

Illustrate and present for a class critique. Ask each student to do a short presentation of his/her rational for the project.

ADVANCED DESIGN PROBLEM

Design a uniform wardrobe for airline flight attendants. Begin by selecting an airline and researching its corporate colors, logo, and philosophy because these must be incorporated into the design of the uniform for a total look. If possible, try to have students interview a flight attendant or invite a guest to class to talk about the physical requirements of the job. Ask for an evaluation of the present uniform and show it to the class. What suggestions would (s)he give a designer creating a new uniform? If possible, ask the flight attendant to return and critique the final presentation of the problem. Uniforms should be a mini-wardrobe build around a mix and match theme so there are several options. Include:

1. outerwear (a coat)
2. serving garment (a pop-over or apron)
3. business-like jacket
4. skirt and pant options
5. blouse, shirt, or other blouse options
6. jumper or dress
7. accessory pieces

Research the uniforms worn by flight attendants on Southwest Airlines. They have a paradigm shift that allows employees to dress in informal sportswear, usually sports and a polo shirt during the summer and khaki slacks and a polo shirt in cooler climates. Does the casual apparel make them seem less competent? Is it more important to have a formal uniform on a flight attendant working on a large airplane equipped for a long-distance flight than on a commuter airline?

These issues are important considerations because each employee reflects the corporate image of the airline and the uniform is the first recognizable indication of how the personality of the business is communicated to its customers.

Fabric selection is very important. Remember that some synthetic fabrics are more combustible than natural fibers and could constitute a fire hazard in an emergency. Garments must be easy care and relatively wrinkle free. Design the uniform with style lines that flatter a wide range of figure types. The variety of temperatures that a flight attendant experiences can be extreme. Their uniforms should be distinctive, but classic enough so they are not dated quickly.

Illustrate and present the project for a class critique.

Vocabulary

Use real life examples and slides to firmly connect the visual definition of the elements and principles of design with actual garments.

28

Acronyms

5 Ws   Who, What, When, Where, Why (also used by journalists)

TEST AND QUIZ QUESTIONS

1. Explain the two major components of the price of a garment. (page 137)

2. What two elements are critical for designing bathing suits? (pages 140-141)

3. Compare and contrast the fit of a jean and a trouser. (pages 142-143 and 146-147)

4. Describe how soft dressing silhouettes help to camouflage figure problems. (pages 146-149)

5. How does the wedge silhouette make a person seem slimmer? (pages 150-151)

6. Which style lines make a person seem taller and slimmer? (pages 157-163)

7. Give two examples of how color can be used for trim or garment color and reinforce the design theme of the outfit. (pages 158-164)

8. Describe the four components of fabric hand. (pages 171-172)

9. What are the three kinds of balance? (pages 175-182)

10. Give an example of a symmetrical and an asymmetrical garment. (pages 179-180)

CHAPTER 5: ORGANIZATION OF A LINE

SUPPLEMENTAL TEACHING INFORMATION

The information in this chapter is closely related to the examples presented in the text's color insert. Building a seasonal color story, grouping fabrics and trims in well-accessorized groups, and developing bodies to complement fabrications are the essence of a designer's job. An individual's success in repeatedly analyzing what is selling and what is new and then synthesizing this information to develop a new product is a critical design skill. The customer "votes" for a successful garment with his/her purchases. The design team's success is dependent on analyzing data, synthesizing information and focusing on the needs of a specific market and creating a product that appeals to a particular customer.

Begin stimulating design students to make decisions by taking them through the actual process. Demonstrate how you would select colors, base goods, accessory fabrics, trims, and bodies, and finally creating a product. The goal in this chapter is to stimulate the students to think of solutions using the information provided. Model how to think through a problem, like selecting a color story and then selecting base goods and accessory fabrics, in front of the students to show them the thinking you want. Create activities that require them to repeat the thought process using a different set of criteria (for example, change the product line from the one used in the class demonstration). In other words, teach critical thinking by demonstrating your thought process by thinking aloud in front of the class. Finally, assess the students' thought processes by requiring them to explain why they made their decisions and allow others to critique their rational.

Require them to:

1. read the material
2. discuss and test their mastery of the vocabulary and basic concepts by discussing and summarizing concepts in class
3. build a color story for a specific product line
4. fabricate the group with base goods and accessory fabrics
5. select trims appropriate in price and style for the fabric groups
6. sketch or demonstrate basic styling themes
7. merchandise styles until they are edited into a salable group

Provide the students with a grab bag of swatches, many of which would "book" into acceptable fabric stories and colors. Include some obvious choices that are inappropriate because of aesthetics, price, or season. Ask the students to divide them into a color story for a specific product and season. Develop a fabric board.

Have each student design a group. Require them to sketch or clip examples from magazines to build the pieces into compatible ensembles or groups styled on a basic theme. Have each student explain his or her project and then do a group critique on each product line. Consider your class carefully and determine if they should work in teams or as individuals. After the critique, ask each student to "buy" items in the groups with "money"—self-adhesive colored dots stuck on the style boards indicating each person's favorites.

Garment Costing

A blank manual cost sheet is included on at the end of this chapter. Make copies and ask the students to complete the line items known to the designer. These include the fabric costs, trim information, and a rough estimate of total material used, and will be the first step in costing a garment. Usually, a production manager uses this information and compares it to similar garments produced in the past to refine the fabric usage and cost of sewing the garment.

A buyer often reverses the process by giving a manufacturer a sample and quoting the purchase price they want to pay. This forces a manufacture to "shop" the garment to a variety of contractors to find the lowest construction cost.

When costing a garment is computerized, the process is more controlled. An example of a computer specification or "spec" sheet is located on text page 211. These documents are used to manage the cost of a garment as it evolves from the estimate to the true cost of producing the first lot and subsequent production versions and reorders.

Bring a garment to class and have the students break down the construction elements and fill in a basic cost sheet to practice the skills necessary to document first cost information.

Color Selection

Collect color prediction kits from fiber companies and color cards from textile firms. Discuss them with your students. They do not have to be current because you are demonstrating color selection, not actually working into a specific fashion cycle. Discuss the hazards of predicting colors far in advance of a season. Evaluate each color selection for appealing colors for your customer as well as colors suitable for the season and fashion trends. Discuss how accurate color predictors were in past seasons? Do they have strengths in specific product areas?

Ask your students to research high fashion European and American designers looking for interesting color ideas. Compare and contrast the information they receive from many sources. Identify color trends and then focus on specific colors that are likely to become seasonal favorites. Remember that some high fashion designers purposely research the color market so they can avoid color trends that are promoted for the mass market. Their aim is to develop a unique product and image to promote their merchandise because they are usually fashion leaders rather than of followers.

Textile Selection Exercise

Collect swatch cards from fabric mills, or, better yet, ask a textile salesperson to visit your class as a guest lecturer. Select color stories from actual swatch cards instead of using predictive services. Ask textile manufacturers to give you old swatch cards and samples from previous seasons to use in class.

Ask the guest lecturer to explain good and bad sampling habits, the importance of committing for duplicate and stock yardage early in the season, and other aspects of appropriate business practices between textile suppliers and manufacturers.

FIELD TRIP RECOMMENDATIONS

Exploring Coordinated Sportswear Groups

Visit a sportswear department in an upscale retail store. Look at a display of coordinated merchandise. Define the theme of the group and identify the color story. Retailers usually select one color from a group and not the entire offering. Competing stores in a trading area may select the same group in different colors. Buyers will often combine garments from several manufacturers that can be mixed-and-matched to create a larger selection. Check to see if all garments on a rounder are from one vendor. Look through the stock and ask sales people to identify the best sellers. These will often be carried in depth (a large selection of sizes and colors). Look at the hanging displays to see how the merchandise has been pulled together to stimulate sales by showing customers how to coordinate pieces as a group.

Sales Rep as a Guest Lecturer

Review a wholesale line with a sales person, a designer, or at a trunk showing. Discuss how the group evolved. Identify garments that are versions of good bodies from previous lines. Which garments are new, fashion-forward bodies? Are there any staples (repeat bodies with classic styling like a basic shirt or simple skirt)? Ask your students to "buy" the merchandise, selecting a group of garments with sufficient tops and bottoms to constitute a group. The ratio is usually 1.5 bottoms to a jacket and 1.5 / 2 soft tops and blouses to one jacket. Discuss buying a classic bottom (trouser or slim skirt) versus a styled bottom. Understanding how a buyer purchases merchandise helps a designer decide what pieces to include in a group.

VISUALS AVAILABLE

Catalogs or sales worksheets are available from a variety of manufacturers. A style sheet is illustrated on page 199 of the text. Many mail order catalogs have mini groups that demonstrate an edited coordinated line. Use these as demonstration pieces to identify themes, color stories, and fabrications.

GENERAL FASHION PROBLEMS

Seasonal Color Stories

Plan color stories that are traditional for the four main seasons: fall, holiday, spring, and summer. Do not consider a specific category of apparel; just pull together traditional color concepts that are fit for each season. Have students work with yarn, fabric swatches, magazines, paint, and Pantone color chips. Use the color insert as a guide to these color selections. Colorists often use dramatic photographs to establish the theme of their color story. Encourage students to use this technique too. Ask the students to name each color and each color story. Designers and merchants have to glamorize their colors stories with romantic names. Have the students mount their color selections neatly on a board. This teaches students how to measure, follow directions, and organize in a logical way. Demonstrate how to use rubber cement:

    a. coat the back of the fabric/color swatch with rubber cement
    b. coat the section of the board that will receive the fabric (plan and mark the area with faint pencil lines or dots)
    c. let the glue dry on both areas
    d. carefully place the swatch on the board with the glued sides contacting each other.

The swatch can be removed and the process repeated if there is an error. Excess glue can be removed with a rubber eraser when dry.

Grade, critique, and display the color boards.

Product Color Stories

Plan color stories for the following specific product areas using available color resources. This is a more sophisticated problem than planning a general color story because it requires market knowledge, a sense of the customer, and research to complete. Require presentation methods similar to those described above.

1. Fall: conservative junior sportswear from a New York line – plan three groups
2. Holiday: evening wear for a New York designer dress house – five groups
3. Spring: contemporary dresses – five groups (where the manufacturer is located is less important in this category because the designer will be most interested in selecting fashionable colors)
4. Summer: California missy swimwear line – three groups
5. Fall/Back to School: children's active wear – two large coordinated sportswear groups

33

MERCHANDISING PROBLEMS

Retail Color Story

Assign each student a separate department in a large store. Ask them to research several groups or classifications of garments from vendors typically included in these areas. Collect and clip photographs from fashion magazines and catalogs to identify colors, fabrics and bodies typically stocked in the departments.

To begin this problem, the student should establish a profile of the target customer answering the 5-Ws to define who-what-when-where-why and how much. List the color stories currently carried in the department and identify the season. Using the collection of scrap, ask each student to create a color story for the department for the next season. Emphasize that color transitions are evolutionary. The customer has to see something new to stimulate his/her desire to purchase another garment, yet have a general frame of reference and basics to have a comfort level with the merchandise. For example, for women, the little black dress is almost always in stock in a dress department.

Again, require students to develop color boards using the format described in the "Seasonal Color Story" exercise. Ask students to present their projects to the class, explaining the customer, current color themes and how they would evolve to the next season. This presentation is typical of a merchandise meeting that a buyer would give to sales people to alert them to new items and color stories. Suggest selling points based on fashion trends students have researched.

BEGINNING CREATIVE PROBLEMS

Resort Sportswear

Design a group of resort/beach wear for spring or summer. Fabricate and develop a color story. Design garments to be sold in resort specialty shops in the better price range. Limit sizes from 4 – 12 (this hint should indicate a more fashionable line). Discuss other places this type of garment might be worn (at home, nightclubs, etc.). Encourage students to investigate innovative fabrications and color combinations, for example, vintage Hawaiian prints. Urge them to visit shops catering to tourists at resort hotels, beach cities, or other vacation destinations. Show clippings of resort garments and research magazines that promote travel and tourism for more ideas.

Dress Group

Assign a dress group as a project. Start beginners with a small group and create a mythical line and designate the season. Ask each student to design 8-10 bodies on separate pieces of paper using simple pencil sketches. Then ask other students to play the role of a merchandise manager in a class critique. Select 4-5 bodies to form the group and model editing skills by discussing why some bodies remain while others are deleted from the group. Ask students to present more formal presentations of the edited groups, complete with rendered sketches and fabric swatches.

Do a final evaluation of the entire class and select groups that would fit together because of color and fabrication for a manufacturer's line for an entire season. Eliminate duplicate fabric stories, selecting the student projects with the most salable bodies, and explain why the selection was made.

Remember to model the thought process you are teaching by "thinking out loud" and encouraging students to discuss their reasons for their design groups and decisions.

ADVANCED CREATIVE PROBLEMS

Long Range Design Problem

Plan and execute (in sketches or samples if time and curriculum warrant) a group for a specific category of apparel. This project makes an excellent final project. It is also appropriate for a team project that simulates a manufacturing organization and allows a talented sales person to team with a designer to develop a product. Assign the category in the second or third week so students have time to grow and develop their ideas during the semester. If the class is a manageable size, have an outside critique.

This should be an exercise in time management as well as creativity and organization. To ensure each student is focusing on developing the project, provide a time line with benchmarks that must be met. Use a project sheet or include the time line in your syllabus.

1. Define the customer, select a company name and design a label and logo.
2. Determine the price line and market. Research fashion trends appropriate for the product.
3. Develop a color story and fabric groups.
4. Sketch many preliminary ideas and discuss them with each student. Merchandise the items, discarding bodies, and adding replacements as necessary before finalizing the line.
5. If this is a team project, separate the team at this point and assign the merchandising student to develop a business plan, research cash flow management and management and marketing. Encourage the design/pattern making student to monitor the product development tasks (samples, style boards, and so forth.) A third student with good technical skills could be added to explore production, shipping, and timing details.
6. Evaluate product development, business, and marketing plans, and production planning. Require the students to plan a presentation where each team member

explains their portion of the project independently—but then require collaboration of the portions of the project that are co-dependent. This process reflects the typical structure of many apparel companies.

Vocabulary

Encourage your students to develop vocabulary lists of the names/phrases used in current "fashion-speak" including:

1. current terms describing fashion trends
2. creative names for colors and styles
3. names of manufacturers from specific markets

Acronyms

8/10 EOM   See definition on text page 215

FOB   Freight On Board – location of a factory warehouse – from this point, shipping charges are calculated to the buyer

TEST AND QUIZ QUESTIONS

1. Describe an item line. (pages 193-194)

2. State three qualifications for a group line. (pages 195-196)

3. Define fashion colors, staples and seasonal colors. (pages 199-202)

4. Describe the role of a designer in developing a cost sheet. (pages 207-210)

5. What are two advantages of a computerized costing system compared with a traditional method? (page 211)

6. Define three components of labor costs in garment construction. (pages 212-213)

7. Describe two methods of determining sewing costs. (page 213)

8. Compare merchandising the cost of a garment with the actual cost of production. (pages 216-217)

9. List two positive aspects of foreign garment production and two negatives. (pages 218-220)

10. What is balanced sourcing? (pages 221-222)

11. Explain the difference between duty and quota. (page 219)

DATE _____ STYLE No. _____

DESCRIPTION _____ SEASON _____

SELLING PRICE: _____

SIZE RANGE _____ COLORS _____ _____

MARKERS _____

MARKER YARDAGE: _____ ALLOWANCE: _____

1. MATERIAL	YARDS	PRICE	AMT.
Lining			

TOTAL MATERIAL COST _____

2. TRIMMINGS	QUANT.	PRICE	AMT.
Buttons			
Pads			
Embroidery			
Belts			
Zippers			
Pleating, Tucking			
Fusing			

TOTAL TRIMMINGS COST _____

3. LABOR	
Cutting	
Labor	
Marking	
Grading	
Payroll Taxes & Health Fund	
Trucking	

TOTAL LABOR COST _____

4. TOTAL COST _____

REMARKS _____

SKETCH

MATERIAL SWATCH

ADAMS PRESS, 830 SO. BROADWAY, L.A. 90014, 627-2151   FORM NO. 32

UNIT TWO
MATERIALS

CHAPTER 6: FABRICATING A LINE

SUPPLEMENTAL TEACHING INFORMATION

Fabric Selection

Invite a fabric salesperson to show a textile line to your class. Ask the students to evaluate the line as if they were designers, taking notes on each fabrication, selecting piece goods to design a specific kind of garment, considering price, delivery details, and minimum purchase requirements to derive a final cost for their garments. Seeing the product "in the mind's eye" is a critical skill for any designer. Before the visit, model this skill by discussing how the hand and surface of the fabric all contribute to the kind of garment that can me made from the fabric. Encourage students to use the following senses:

- Visual – look at the fabric and imagine what a garment made in the textile would look like
- Touch or *hand* – feel the finish and texture of the fabric and imagine how it would drape and feel when worn in a variety of climates
- Intellect – ask the textile sales person about the care necessary to maintain the fabric, technical production issues like shrinkage, pressing sewing techniques, and so forth.
- Economics – is the assortment (colors, finishes, patterns) appropriate for the line? Is the cost and delivery schedule a fit for the product? Can the fabric be customized to complement other fabrics in the group and so forth?

Develop an information sheet and require students to use the format for note taking as the salesperson shows the line so all critical information is covered.

Ask the salesperson the best way a designer can review a textile line. In addition to the usual sales pitch, ask for the specialties of the fabric company and a brief history. What are the terms of purchase? Usually textiles are sold on "60-net" terms. This means if payment is not made within 60 days of the receipt of goods, the manufacturer may have to pay interest on the balance owed. Textile companies evaluate the purchase by reviewing the manufacturer's credit and reputation. If no credit history exists, a new manufacturer may have to pay for the fabric COD (collect on delivery.) Often there is a small discount for COD payment. Ask the sales person to describe current trends in the textile market and future directions in the economy, technology, and sales practices that will influence the textile market.

Writing a Sample Order

The format of a sample order differs from company to company, but standard information is common to all order blanks. A small manufacturer may use a standard form printed for many other companies, but most large firms customize the fabric ordering form adding specific terms and conditions. In an emergency, the fabric company can provide an order blank. It is important to fill out all the sections completely, not only to ensure the correct delivery of the samples selected, but also to create a guide for future ordering of the fabric if it is used in the line. The following information is especially important:

1. resource information (vendor address, sales person, address, phone, fax)
2. style and color numbers
3. fabric description, fiber content, unusual care instructions
4. technical details including width, weights, minimum yardage requirements for customized colors and prints
5. shipping details including delivery information for stock yardage, cancellation date for sample shipping, rush shipping instructions, and so forth.

Provide each student with an information sheet and review the facts that should be included to accurately write sample and stock orders. Require them to take notes during a fabric presentation.

Ask the students to use their notes to write a sample order. Check the details and highlight the items that are not complete. Grade this exercise.

Finally, provide students with another order form and require them to write a duplicate yardage order using their notes and the sample order for information. Refer to the calendar in earlier chapters to determine the appropriate shipping dates. Establish a specific number of duplicate samples ordered and require students to estimate the yardage that will be required to cut a complete set of duplicates.

Emphasize the importance of completing each step of this process accurately. Mistakes cost money that could compromise a designer's job.

Buying Knit Fabrics

Cotton and cotton blend knits (interlock and jersey) are priced by the pound instead of the yard. This is important because the characteristics of knit fabric change during the finishing and knitting process and may seem heavier than they really are. Knowing the amount of yarn in each yard of fabric ensures that it is not being altered during the finishing process.

Yarns are sold and dyed by the pound. Knitters compute variations in price in terms of pounds. To change the pound price to yards (necessary to compute marker yardage, etc.) use the following formula:

Price per pound divided by the yield + price per yard

Example: $3.50 per pound divided by 1.80 yards of fabric = $1.94 per yard

Yield is the amount of yardage produced by one pound of yarn and depends on how large the yarn is, how tightly it is knit, the type of stitch and how the fabric is finished. Knits are also described by weight. For example, a 7-ounce interlock has about 7 ounces of yarn per yard.

Textile Sales

Textile firms encourage manufacturers to commit for fabrics ahead of the season. The textile converter can better plan the greige goods commitments if they have an idea of what the large cutters will be ordering. It is especially important to contract (commit for future delivery) for a textile purchase when there is a factor that limits supply. Wool is a good example of a fiber that has limited production. The sales representatives solicit contracts for the amount of fiber that the company has purchased for the coming season. When the fiber or greige goods is gone the textile is "sold up" for that period. As more fiber becomes available, the market opens up. To be sure of a supply, a manufacturer purchase future production from the mill.

Usually, the year is divided into quarters and the textile converter sells production in three-month periods. A sales person may say their line will "open up in the third quarter" meaning that more goods will be available in July and can only be sold currently if the manufacturer is willing to take a "position," that is, purchase now for delivery during the third quarter of the year.

Velvet and corduroy are two fabrics that require special machines to weave and finish the goods. These machines are limited in number and cannot be converted to manufacture other fabrics. Therefore, velvet and corduroy are typical allotment fabrics that must be purchased on a "program" over several quarters of the year.

Denim is often on allotment. The large jeans manufacturers in the United States (Levi, VF Corporation makers of Wrangler and Lee brands, Guess? and others) purchase the bulk of domestically produced denim, and small cutters may have difficulty getting contracts for the remaining production. One solution is to buy foreign piece goods. Distressed finishes, which require washing and other treatments, also limit the fabric available because of the extra process and the limited capacity of available machines.

Assorting or deciding on the color or print for the base goods can be done closer to the season if the manufacturer has a contract with a converter. Assorting the fabric depends on the manufacturing process and is discussed on pages 228-230 of the text

Textile producers are confronted with a tight financial market and require manufacturers to commit to purchases earlier and earlier. Mills cannot afford to produce sample and duplicate yardage without contracts from manufacturers. This is a problem for small manufacturers, especially when they are in an experimental, high fashion niche market because they cannot anticipate how a garment or group will sell and make accurate projections to purchase fabric until they have orders and ship the goods.

FIELD TRIP RECOMMENDATIONS

Plan a trip to a primary fabric source. This kind of trip depends on where you are located. Rural areas may be centers of cotton production. The southern United States and New England are particularly rich sources of primary textile producers. These include:

1. The south and east coast – specialty fabrics (cotton, velvet, etc.), knitting mills, finishers, spinners, dyers, and printers
2. The south, California and Texas – cotton fields and gins, spinners, cotton cooperatives (especially in the rural south, California's San Joaquin Valley and Imperial Valley, many parts of Texas)
3. Southern California, northeast US – finishers, printers, knitters, and embroidery factories (especially in New Jersey where factories are often family businesses located in garages), mills, weavers, and commercial laundries that distress denim.
4. Other locations – specialty printers and other operations that can demonstrate textile crafts to your students.

When you visit a textile producer, ask for information on product development, how styles and designs are produced, problems associated with acquiring yarn, restrictions related to environmental issues, labor problems, and so forth, to better understand the constraints of the production process.

Prior to the 1990s, most large fiber producers had libraries consisting of swatches of fabric made from their fiber. Designers and manufacturers were encouraged to visit and learn about the latest textile trends and resources. Many libraries no longer exist, victims of years of budget cuts. Cotton Inc. still maintains libraries in both New York and Los Angeles. These valuable resources allow a designer to get an overview of the market and check European and domestic fabric, fashion and color trends at no cost.

Textile trade shows are also resources for the market. Foreign converters often use these trade shows to promote their goods. Students are often welcome to visit these shows. Check with organizers before planning a field trip. Learn about these shows from trade newspapers and web sites.

GENERAL FASHION PROBLEMS

Textile Hand

Demonstrate how different fabrics drape. Bring extreme examples of the following kinds of textiles to class and drape them on a dress form or body to show your students what fabric hand and finish really means:

Crisp hand	Organza (light weight)
	Taffeta (medium weight)
	Linen (heavy suiting weight)

Compare and contrast silhouettes and characteristics with:

Soft hand	Silk or micro fiber jersey (light weight knit)
	Silk or rayon crepe de chine (light weight woven)
	Jersey, wool, or acrylic (medium weight knit)
	Crepe (medium weight woven)
	Knit velour (heavy weight knit)
	Wool crepe (heavy weight woven)

Demonstrate how the fabric conforms or resists the body's contour by draping on the dress form. Discuss how the had affects styling and involve students by asking them to suggest silhouettes appropriate for each fabrication. Also drape the fabrics on the bias grain and compare the effect to the straight grain. A reference (with visuals if possible) to present how the Paris designers Vionette and Gres used bias grain would be very appropriate here. Consult the book, *Couture, An Illustrated History of the Great Paris Designers and Their Creations* by Ruth Lynam (Doubleday and Company, New York, 1972).

Denim Hand

Compare and contrast unwashed denim with pre-washed. Discuss the live style that encourages the use of pre-washed fabrics to obtain a soft, used look to new clothes. Should the styling be different for pre-washed denims in fashion items? Does the faded quality of the indigo dye enhance the aesthetics of pre-washed fabric?

Incorporate the denim experiment into a creative design problem by asking your students to design traditional and contemporary garments using unwashed and pre-washed denim fabrics. Incorporate the differences between the crisp and soft hand of the two fabric finishes into the design. Use the excellent text and visuals from *American Denim, A New Folk Art* by Richard Owens, Tony Lane and Paul Beagle (Harry N. Abrams, Inc. New York).

42

MERCHANDISING PROBLEMS

Assign various members of the class to specific product categories and ask them to research textiles used by vendors in the classification. You may ask them to select a category (a snag here is many will want junior apparel if you have a young class) or have the students draw the categories randomly. This method of selection provides each student with a separate topic and no exchange of work is possible.

Typical categories are:

1. Children's wear – 3 to 6x, moderate price
2. Boys wear – 7 to 14, chain store products
3. Missy dresses – bridge departments
4. Contemporary sportswear – moderate

Divide the students among stores that are available in your teaching area and send them to shop and compile the following information:

1. kinds of fabric found in regular stock
2. season
3. exceptional fabrications that look new and exciting
4. fabric in the expensive and lower ends of the department pricing structure
5. prominent colors
6. ratio of patterns to plain goods
7. emphasis on easy care or durability in the category
8. range of fibers use—are natural or synthetics emphasized?
9. name the vendors that seem the most forward versus those that provide staples

The format of the problem can be expanded into a unit project if your students are asked to compare the textiles used in several categories of merchandise. For example:

> Compare and contract missy fabrications in designer, better, moderate and budget departments in one store. Describe how budged and moderate fabrications compare to those found in a chain store.

BEGINNING DESIGN PROBLEMS

Print Dress Designs

Select a simple figurative print and have your students recolor the print.

- Select new colors for the print using yarns, paint chips, or fabric swatches to experiment with color combinations.
- Try several different ground colors including with or off white, black and navy.

- Trace the print using vellum or tracing paper and carefully recolor the print using paint, felt pens, or transparent dyes.

Demonstrate the recolor process on a CAD program. Run through many color ways. Time the process of hand painted croquis and compare them to the CAD options. This is a good project for a class critique.

Combining Geometric Fabric Patterns

Use traditional seersucker stripes to create a group of summer garments. Consider possible fabric combinations (tiny gingham checks, delicate florals, etc.) and trim the base goods to enhance the group. Plan a color story and design a coordinated sportswear group of 8 to 12 pieces.

Children's Summer Dress Group

Design a group of summer dresses for a dress line appealing to girls, size 3 to 6x, using gingham checks. The group should consist of three or four pieces that are offered in several colors. Fabrications could include:

- Combine several different size checks in one color
- Combine one size check in different colors
- Combine eyelet with gingham
- Combine simple geometric prints (dots, stripes, etc.) with gingham
- Use trims to make the gingham distinctive (appliqués, embroidery, ric rac, and ribbons).

ADVANCED DESIGN PROBLEMS

How Interfacings Work

Investigate interfacings and collect a wide range of demonstration types and garments they are used in. Collect many weights of non-woven interfacings produced by the Pellon Corporation. Request pamphlets and other visuals from your local distributor and share them with your students. Pellon has several excellent product videos. Shop commercial garments and see what interfacings are used and how they perform. Are fusible or sew-in interfacings used?

Demonstrate hand-padding techniques typically used in better men's wear. Discuss hymo, tailor's cloth, and other underpinnings of traditionally tailored garments. Take the lining out of a man's suit and expose the hand padding stitches and show how traditional tailoring techniques shape a jacket. Compare and contrast traditional techniques with fusible currently used for moderate and less expensive garments.

Assign the students a soft-hand wool double knit fabric and ask them to design a series of structured jackets that incorporate crisp tailoring details as well as the soft drape natural to the fabric. Emphasize style lines, and a variety of sleeve and lapel treatments.

Print Fabric Exercise

Select a specific merchandise category and ask your students to design a print appropriate for that customer. Provide a variety of ideas that can be developed into prints (flowers, leaves, animals, geometrics, ethnic motifs, and so forth) that can be worked into a design. Discuss the reasons for using specific printing methods for the various effects possible.

Show students a variety of layouts, discuss the way a motif is repeated to create certain effects and relate the scale of the print to the human body. Have the students try several layouts for their motifs—one way; staggering the design; spacing variations; and so forth. Require each student recolor the print into several color-ways. Work up at least five preliminary ideas and select the most promising for the final croquis.

Large Scale Prints

Clip photographs of bed sheets from advertisements or editorials in glossy shelter magazines and store catalogs. Look for large, bold designs. Ask your students to design at-home garments using the sheets. Collect samples of ethnic djellabas and caftans as inspirations for the bodies. Emphasize the advantage of extra-wide fabrics and require the students to eliminate as many seams as possible. Use the large-scale graphics found on many sheets to create a dramatic garments.

Better Lace Construction

Lace dresses that have been custom made or constructed by couture houses are seamed by cutting out the lace patterns and hand sewing them together so there are no obvious seams. Self-edging scallops are often used to decorate hems and necklines. This is an expensive way to construct lace garments, but one with high aesthetic values. Collect vintage lace garments as examples. Museum collections usually have good examples. Discuss machine-made laces and compare them with those made by hand.

Suggest using hand-made imported handkerchiefs, tea towels, table clothes, or pillowcases to make garments or parts of garments, combining a hand-made look with a commercially produced garment. Ask the students to design a lace dress using traditional seams and one that is a custom made, hand-fitted lace garment.

Solid and Print Designs

Clip examples of solid and print fabric combinations used in one garment. Look for high fashion examples of fabric combinations. Koos Vander Acker is a New York designer who combines several prints, trims, and fabrics in custom designs. Look for examples of his work to inspire students to combine multiple fabrics in a single garment.

Ask your students to collect a variety of fabrics, perhaps combining antique pieces and ethnic textiles with commercial fabrics. Design garments using three or more prints and textiles in one ensemble or garment. The final presentation should have swatches of fabric mounted with the design. Consider using trims like ribbons, lace, and bias bindings to transition the fabrics. This project is excellent for stimulating creativity and should be evaluated on innovation.

VOCABULARY

The primary goal of this chapter is to synthesize textile names with actual fabrications. Collect textiles and show them to your students so they can build their verbal, tactile and visual vocabulary of textile terms.

Acronyms

COD	Collect On Delivery
PFP	Prepared For Print

TEST AND QUIZ QUESTIONS

1. Explain the difference between a vertical mill and a converter. (page 235)

2. Describe the sales terms that position textile mills in the role of financing apparel manufacturers. (pages 228-229)

3. What is the responsibility of an apparel designer when reviewing fabric lines to sample for the next season? (pages 228-230)

4. Explain how the textile production process determines minimum yardage requirements? (pages 236-238)

5. Name and describe two commercial resources for textile information. (pages 240-243)

6. Name/describe the four characteristics that define a textile. (pages 243-245)

7. How is digital printing process going to change the textile sampling process? (page 237)

Mill Name _____

Address _____ City/Zip Code _____

New York Contact _____ Phone _____

Los Angeles Rep. _____ Phone _____

Season _____

Name of Pattern #	Fiber Content	Price	Width	Delivery & Comment

CHAPTER 7: KINDS OF TRIMS AND THEIR USES

SUPPLEMENTAL TEACHING INFORMATION

The most valuable tool for lecturing on the material in this chapter is a collection of trims. Your collection can be gathered from the following sources:

1. make your own examples
2. acquire old clothes that have unique trims
3. ask students to donate good projects
4. collect from suppliers, other instructors, and community sources such as museums and private collectors
5. ask manufacturers for donations of old sample cards
6. assign students to bring in specific examples
7. ask your friends to remember your collection when they clean out their closets

As your collection grows, organize it in groups of trims and use contemporary and period garments to illustrate specific points. Gather photographs and actual samples, label them appropriately and put them in students' hands so they can feel the trim as you describe it. Lecture on sources, costs associated with specific trims, appropriate end products, care compatibility issues, and so forth.

Art-to-wear and hand made one-of-a-kind-garments are naturals to explore in connection with this chapter. Invite designers who craft this category of garment to speak to your students. Ask them to cover the economic as well as the aesthetic aspects of this specialized product.

FIELD TRIP RECOMMENDATIONS

The following suggestions are appropriate for this chapter as well as for Chapter 6, because they illustrate both textiles and trims.

1. museums and regional historical societies
2. vintage clothing dealers
3. private collections
4. Goodwill and Salvation Army collections and stores
5. handicraft artisans

Some collectors will not allow their garments to be handled or worn. This makes studying the garments difficult. A body in clothing makes the garment come alive. Particularly good collections are often found at Goodwill and historical societies. These institutions have valuable items of clothing donated for study purposes.

Consider starting your own collection of garments. I did so, using the tax-free status of the college where I worked to encourage prominent community members to donate apparel annually. Each donor establishes the value of the items they donate and receive a form and thank-you letter that confirms the donation and its value so they may claim the donation as an income tax deduction. The collection expanded rapidly as faculty members began to see the value of real-life examples. The college dedicated a storage facility to the collection that has a small lecture area so students can look at examples of design, trims, and fabric treatments in comfort, and the pieces do not have to leave the room. A separate collection of textiles, trims, and laces is an important resource to build the visual and verbal vocabulary of students.

Consider visiting trim contractors with a camera in hand and take photographs of the specialized machines used to create trims. Usually these factories are small places and cannot handle groups of students. Devise a slide or power point lecture that demonstrates the machine and the type of trim it makes. Invite a trim salesperson to give a lecture to your students.

Collect craft books and share them with your class. There is a wealth of ideas available for appliqué patterns, embroideries, and quilts. Needlepoint books can suggest fabric patterns. Reprints of old Sears catalogs are filled with examples of period trim details.

GENERAL FASHION PROBLEMS

Require your students to find and describe two or three examples of each category of trims you have discussed in a photograph, magazine clip, or actual item. Have them organize this information in a notebook or display board.

MERCHANDISING PROBLEM

Children's Wear Trims

Shop department stores, specialty stores, and catalogs that carry children's wear. Compile a scrapbook or clipping file of trimmed garments. Compare the type and amount of trimming details found in similar garment silhouettes at different price points. Evaluate the durability of the trim on several garments to determine if it detracts from the care of the item.

Cartoon-based Apparel

Compare the design and merchandising approach used to promote the "Winnie the Pooh" collection with another popular line in the same price range. Assign a comparison of children's wear carried by the Disney stores versus the Warner Brother's selection. Consider price, fabrications, colors, trims, presentation of the merchandise, fit, assortment, and the total appeal of the garments.

Does the image of the cartoon characters make the apparel particularly appealing? Retailers and manufactures must pay a royalty and be licensed to use the commercial images created by a studio or cartoon artist. Does the appeal of the merchandise compensate for the added cost?

Intimate Apparel

Compare and contrast the merchandise sold by Victoria's Secret, a specialty store and catalog—often called a *category killer* because the dominate a particular retail category with a wide and deep concentration of merchandise---with a lingerie department in a large store.

1. list the kinds of merchandise each retailer carries
2. evaluate the "depth" of the stock; that is, the range of sizes and colors available in each style
3. note the "width" or variety of styles available in each category
4. compare the quality of trims, elastic, and details on the merchandise in each store
5. compare and contrast the display methods and ambiance of both retailers

Relate lingerie to the prevailing silhouette trends in outerwear. Do fashion foundations enhance the clothing worn over them? Does there seem to be a time lag between trends in outerwear and intimate apparel designed to compliment it? Are their fashion trends unique to intimate apparel? Are lingerie fashions compatible with current lifestyles? Think of today's emphasis on a natural bosom and "wonder bra" styles compared with the rigid, pointed breasts typical of the 1950s. Compare the push-up wonder bras to sports bras.

Each apparel category has style trends, unique color stories, trims, and fabrications that evolve through the fashion cycle. Studying these trends is the first step to understanding how the product is designed.

BEGINNING DESIGN PROBLEMS

T-shirt Decoration

Assign a T-shirt design project requiring students to design hand-painted motifs for a basic shirt. Discuss how funky designs (surfer or motorcycle images) appeal to specialized groups first and often become popular with mainstream customers. Ask the students to research video games or tattoos as inspiration for design motifs. Sketch the design on paper, selecting the best design. Stretch the T-shirt over a board and reproduce the image using waterproof markers, textile paints, or dyes. Display the shirts on models of have the students wear them to a critique.

Girl's Sleepwear

Design sleepwear for girls (sizes 7–14) using trims as the primary design theme.

1. design two garments for summer and two for winter
2. select fabrics and colors appropriate for each season
3. use four or more of the following trims on garments:

appliqués	lace edging	braids
ribbons	ruffles	fabric combinations
elastic	shirring or smocking	quilting
embroidery		

Sketch the garments and present them on an illustration board with fabric and trim swatches.

ADVANCED CREATIVE PROBLEM

Trimmed Man's Shirt Project

Modify a classic man's shirt as a quick trim project. Ask each student to bring a white, long-sleeved man's shirt that can be cut up and decorated. These can be purchased for very little at a second hand store if none are available at home. Give students a limited amount of time to modify and trim the shirt. Encourage them to cut, fit, paint, add trims, and otherwise decorate the shirt. You may provide a variety of donated trims or ask the students to come in with grab bags of their own. Critique and model the designs at the end of the project.

Denim Trim Project

Using a remarkable book, *American Denim, A New Folk Art* by Beagle, Owens, and Lane (Harry N. Abrams, Inc., New York, 1975) as inspiration, assign students classic denim garments such as jeans and jackets to trim. *American Denim* has wonderful color visuals incorporating painting, embroidery, quilting, studding, appliqués, trapunto, and distressed fabrics. Students can be required to sketch their designs or actually make them.

Study commercial denim garments sold from 1960s to the present. Note how trims have come to dominate the commercial market.

Folk Costume Inspiration

Base a project on research of a folk culture and their costumes. Require students to read, research, view examples, and document their findings. Use this as a basis for designing contemporary garments inspired by the trim and structure of the ethnic costumes.

Note how often folk costume has inspired haute couture and designer garments during the last decades of the twentieth century. Trace Yves St. Laurent's evolution noting the influence of ethnic costume in his designs.

As a companion project, require students to design garments that do not use conventional zippers, snaps or buttons. Require that the garments be wrapped, sashed, or tied. Integrate the fastenings into the design of the garments. Ask students to consider using knits or stretch fabrics.

Collect photographs of ethnic costumes that have evolved from rectangular pieces of fabric and are shaped to the body without using darts and gores typical of conventional Western apparel. Look at Japanese and Chinese garments for inspiration. Stress creative solutions to this problem.

This theoretical problem often becomes a practical one when designers work in underdeveloped countries and cannot import zippers and buttonhole machines. Once, when designing a junior sportswear line in India, I used brass harness bells (with the clapper removed!) instead of buttons as fastenings for a group. The commercial button selection was very unattractive and I had to invent a new fastening from available materials.

SCHOOL CONTEST

Create a Creation

This contest was developed by Joyce Gale, an instructor at the Fashion Center, Los Angeles Trade-Technical College, and has been used to stimulate the creativity of students for many years.

Solicit donations of trims and fabric. If fabric is not available, purchase enough of a basic fabrication (approximately 1 ½ yards per person) to design a top. Charge each student $5 - $10 for a bag of "ingredients." Each set of ingredients should have the same amount of trims and base goods. Students may only add thread and imagination.

Collect the entry funds approximately two weeks before the bags of identical ingredients are distributed. Include the rules for the contest.

1. Design a garment for the top portion of the body using only the items in the bag, with the exception of sewing thread
2. Not all fabric and trim must be used
3. Creativity is the most important ingredient
4. Due date (give students at least three weeks)

52

Display the creations. Invite judges from industry or the community to vote on the most creative. Award scholarships, certificates, awards, etc. This is a study in how creative designers can be when solving a problem and how many different solutions are possible, even though everyone starts with the same ingredients.

VOCABULARY

The challenge with the trim chapter parallels the chapter on textiles; students must connect the visual image of an item with its name and envision how the trim can be used. Consider testing students by providing photographs of trimmed garments and asking them to identify all the items used.

TEST AND QUIZ QUESTIONS

1. Name three of the five rules for selecting an appropriate trim. (page 257)

2. Name the four styling factors that determine how a collar looks and diagram a lapel collar and label the components of the collar. (page 259)

3. Describe two methods for making a rigid belt. (pages 267-268)

4. What kinds of belts can be made in house? (pages 267-268)

5. What are the guidelines for pocket placement in pairs? (pages 270-271)

6. Name five kinds of pockets and sketch them. (pages 271-273)

7. Name and describe five materials often used for buttons. (pages 275-276)

8. Name, sketch, and describe three button shapes. (page 277)

9. Describe typical button placement for tops and shirts. (pages 278-280)

10. Describe three fastenings (other than zippers and buttons) used on garments. (pages 281-283)

11. Name five linear trims. (page 285)

12. Name two kinds of ruffles. (pages 288-290)

13. Describe three kinds of area trims. (pages 292-295)

14. Describe three trims often used on children's wear. (pages 295)

UNIT THREE
SPECIALITY DESIGN CATEGORIES

CHAPTER 8: CHILDREN'S WEAR

SUPPLEMENTARY TEACHING INFORMATION

Customer Research

Creating specialized merchandise requires customer research. A focus group allows manufacturers to investigate the requirements of a customer prior to creating merchandise or an advertising campaign. This research is especially important when identifying trends that are driving a fast-changing market driven by group dynamics like the youth market. A focus groups works this way:

Target Markets

Identify the customer profile for a specific apparel category. For example, when determining who purchases apparel for toddlers through sizes 6x, the focus group would be parents. Pre-teens have definite opinions on fashion and a focus group for this category should be made of children ages 7 to 12. Focus group members should fit the profile of a typical customer for the product. Usually, participants are paid a small fee.

Formulate a series of questions that identify specific information that will help product development and merchandising teams to develop a successful line. Product is often shown to participants so they have a specific frame of reference. Reviewing samples provides true insight into styling, color selection, and fabric preferences. Divide your class and ask it to assume the role of participants and organizers of a focus group. Questions should cover the following items:

- Color preference
- Pricing
- Fabric preference
- Style questions
- Fit requirements
- Care requirements
- Retail outlets preferred
- Periodicals and advertisements

Cooperate with a local nursery school or your campus childcare center to set up a true focus group after you have practiced. Design students may even have children evaluate their designs and children's wear garments from a construction project.

Compile and numerically evaluate the results so conclusions can be statistically analyzed. Video taping the actual focus group provides an additional analytic tool.

Marketing research firms use focus groups for a great variety of products and marketing strategies. Usually creating apparel season after season is so demanding and continuous that a designer does not have time or resources to do primary research for each line. A manufacturer should research a potential market prior to starting a new line or fine-tune a product offering using primary research like a focus group.

A designer should constantly research product requirements informally. For children's wear, this requires observing children at school, play, and social events. Informal discussions with parents and children are also helpful. In addition, specialty products like sleepwear are covered by government regulations requiring special testing for textile flammability and labeling. A manufacturer in these categories has to be very aware of regulations.

Retailers are a valuable resource for product development information. They are quick to spot a void in the market and often approach a manufacturer with special products or lines. Care must be taken to avoid a short-term product run, as start-up costs can eat into profits.

Many manufacturers are successful because they perceive a void in the market based on their own experience. They must create a niche, that is, develop a unique offering at a price acceptable in the market place and then publicize their product to a sufficient amount of stores or customers to create the volume necessary to start a business and keep it growing. Often publicity is the key to accelerating the demand for a product. Constant contact with the trade and consumer press keeps the name of the line or the designer in front of the buying public. Free coverage in the press is called public relations. Paid advertising often encourages reporters to cover the line and results in some free editorial coverage in trade publications.

GENERAL FASHION PROBLEMS

Select a specific category of children's wear, focusing on a size range sold at a specific type of retailer (for example: boys', sizes 3 to 6x – sold in department stores.)

Isolate two distinctive areas of this category, active wear and special occasion clothes. Identify the following silhouettes, fabrics, and items in the category and compare and contrast the price for each item:

1. basic items
2. fabrics used
3. color stories
4. fashion treatments
5. names of major vendors

Now compare and contrast the same points with a retailer known as a "category killer." These specialty retailers seek to dominate a market. The merchandise is often knocked off from major fashion lines at a lower price. Children's wear specialists include Children's GAP, Bass, Old Navy, OshKosh, and other retailers.

MERCHANDISING PROBLEM

Evaluate a children's wear specialty store by comparing it to departments in a chain store (Sears, Penny's, Wal Mart, etc.) and a department store. Look for upscale children's wear specialists like the mall stores catering to bubble-gum juniors (pre- and young teen age girls) and compare and contrast the following:

1. décor and interior design of the stores
2. sales personnel
3. credit practices
4. stock: lines carried, amount of stock, depth of assortment, ability to special order, special promotions and sale items, size ranges, special events, advertising
5. location
6. facilities for children (play areas, toys, etc.)

List the positive and negatives of each situation. Carefully consider the subjective differences (price, stock, size range) and the objective differences (atmosphere, personality, amenities, designer labels) and outline the kinds of customers each retailer attracts.

BEGINNING DESIGN PROBLEMS

Figure Problems

List and sketch the figure problems that children in the 3–14 size range often have. Sketch a variety of simple silhouettes and bodies that camouflage each figure problem. Consider using color, proportion, and line to minimize each problem.

School Uniform

Design a uniform line for grammar school children. Concentrate on adapting pieces from sportswear lines that are comfortable and easy to produce. Research fabrics and determine the standards for this market. Design enough pieces to adapt to a wide range of temperatures.

Novelty Tops

Design a series of novelty tops for children. Research current "hot personalities" (cartoon characters, super heroes, television stars – both real and animated) and select a theme.

Develop graphic images from your theme that would be appropriate for embroidery or screening on sweatshirts, novelty tops and T-shirts. A more advanced project would have each student develop an original "theme" or character. A good example is the Big Dog sportswear line for young men and boys.

Illustrate and mount all designs on board for a formal critique.

ADVANCED DESIGN PROBLEMS

Historic Children's Wear as Inspiration

Research historic children's wear. To find these examples, look at past fashion magazines, fine art examples of children, old store catalogs (Sears are reprinted), and period children's books. Sketch the most important examples in your sketchbook.

Research contemporary fabrics, searching for examples that would translate into styling for girls special occasion dresses (sizes 3–6x or 7–14) based on historic details. Pay particular attention to the shapes and details you have found. Adapt the research—do not use it line for line. Shop current children's lines that are based on nostalgia and vintage apparel like Laura Ashley.

Sketch a group of garments using at least three colors of base goods or print fabrics and a selection of bodies based on the vintage theme. Mount on illustration board and critique the project.

Children's Swim Wear

Design a series of bathing suits for young girls. Start with a group of prints that are based on one or more of the following themes:

1. fruit prints
2. animal prints
3. nautical geometrics
4. exotic birds

Design the basic prints for three groups. Each should have a distinct color theme. Plan the scale (size of the print) keeping in mind the size of the front of a child's one-piece bathing suit. Bathing suit designers usually use a large paper template the size and shape of the front of a one-piece suit placed over a print to quickly evaluate how to place the motif on a suit.

Design the bodies for each print group. Each group should include at least one two-piece suit, a one-piece suit, and a novelty like a tankini. Design a cover up for each group. Usually the same print would be used, but printed on a less expensive base goods than Lycra spandex—the typical bathing suit fabrication.

VOCABULARY

Emphasize current trends in popular entertainment culture that target children. Discuss current hot movies, cartoon characters, comic book heroes, and television personalities that appeal to children.

TEST AND QUIZ QUESTIONS

1. What are the two largest categories of children's apparel? (pages 305-306)

2. What season is most important for gift-giving apparel? (page 307)

3. Name four items typically included in spring children's wear lines. (pages 307-308)

4. What is the most frequently used fiber for children's wear and why? (page 310)

5. Why are pure polyester fabrics undesirable for children's wear? (page 311)

6. What are the two most widely used decorative trims used for children's wear? (pages 312-313)

7. What are the main size ranges for children's wear? (pages 318 and 332)

8. How is infant's wear displayed in a store or showroom? (page 322)

9. What magazines influence young children and pre-teen girls' apparel selections? (page 331)

CHAPTER 9: MEN'S WEAR

SUPPLEMENTAL TEACHING INFORMATION

Men's business wear (suits, sports coats, long sleeve dress shirts and ties) has very subtle styling. Tailors most often design formal business suits, virtually eliminating a "designer" per se. A tailor adapts basic cuts, helps select fabric, and is an expert on fit and construction. A tailor most often directs product development for large commercial suit manufacturers.

Designing men's tailored clothing involves recognition of styling details and current fabric trends. Tailored men's wear tends to change very slowly—evolutionary changes rather than the revolutionary changes typical of women's wear. Significant styling changes usually originate in Europe at the high-end designer level and gradually the most wearable runway fashions filter into daily wear. To illustrate this for your students, collect suits. Show the students the subtle detailing typical of a hand tailored suit by removing the lining and exploring the inner structure of the garment. Compare conservative men's wear with high fashion lines such as Armani and Cerruti.

The fashion cycle is very different in men's sportswear. In this market, merchandise techniques popularized in the women's sportswear area have permeated this much more volatile fashion category. Designers are often women and trends are more important than traditional details and structure. Fashion is an ever-changing element in sportswear development. Fabric and color combinations are more important than radical silhouette changes. Many men's wear designers travel Europe and the Orient to research styling details. Shape changes more slowly than in women's wear and, of course, the radical changes in proportion created by hemlines are non-existent in men's wear.

FIELD TRIP RECOMMENDATIONS

Custom Tailor Shop

Arrange a trip to a local tailor. There are custom tailor shops in most medium- and large-size cities. Ask the tailor to describe how a tailored jacket is constructed. Demonstrate how to measure a customer and how a basic jacket and pant block is adjusted to the figure variations of an individual. Ask the tailor to discuss the subtle differences in styling and how they can minimize figure problems. Discuss fabric selection and how subtle variations in weight, pattern, and texture relate to seasons and the style of a sports coat or suit.

Men's Wear Retail Store

If you are able, visit a large men's wear fashion retailer. Barney's New York is the ultimate example of a store dedicated to almost every type and most price ranges of men's wear. Nordstrom also has an extensive men's apparel division. Macy's New York is famous for their selection of men's apparel.

Ask the public relations department or a merchandise specialist for a tour. Ask the representative to discuss the profile of customers who frequent each department. Match manufacturers to each department and customer. Ask for an explanation of the subtle differences between the vast assortment of suits offered so your students can understand the role fabric and construction details play in the selection and design of a man's suit.

Ask how accessories are tied into each phase of the business and how they bridge the types of suits offered. Ask for information on current "hot" neckwear colors and patterns.

Ask students to write a field-trip report on the event.

GENERAL FASHION PROBLEM

Vintage Men's Wear Inspiration

Research a decade of men's active wear fashion between 1900 and 1950. Collect pictures of active sportswear garments from the period. Be sure to research European fashions as well as American apparel. Look in publications covering sporting events from these periods. Pay particular attention to these sports:

Golf	Polo	Skiing
Sailing/marine sports	Hunting	Baseball
Tennis	Surfing	Western equestrian wear
Soccer	Rugby	

Draw parallels between current sportswear styling and period examples. Look for details, items and the shape of the clothes. Trace the evolution of various items. Try to discover items that would translate to a contemporary man's wardrobe with some modification.

MERCHANDISING PROBLEMS

Brand Identification

Shop several large department or chain stores. List the national brands carried in the men's sportswear departments. Compare the branded manufacturers to the merchandise made for the store. Is the store brand confined to basics (business shirts, underwear, basic T-shirts, pants?) Is the branded merchandise also available for young men?

Compare merchandise from the same vendor carried in several different stores. Is the assortment different? Compare price points and identify differences. Do both retailers carry the same depth of stock and sizes? Identify the top 4-5 manufactures in both stores and estimate their importance to the retailer.

Specialty Store Merchandising

Shop an expensive men's wear specialty shop. Walk into the store and try to guess the price range of the merchandise before checking out labels and price tags. Is the image of the store consistent with the merchandise presented?

Do the sales people reflect the image of the ideal customer? Are they dressed in the merchandise featured in the store? Does the store cater to one life style or do they have several departments that obviously try to attract a variety of age ranges and life styles?

What special services does the store offer to make shopping more appealing? Check out the "hidden services" like credit, alterations, gift-wrapping, and credit policies. Is there a clubroom or bar available for customers? What other amenities attract the customer? Is pricing a factor that makes up for the lack of amenities and services? What kind of music does the store play?

Compare and contrast the image projected by an upscale specialty store with a men's wear retailer catering to teen-age boys. Consider all the factors that attracted an older, up-scale man to a specific store and contrast them with what appeals to a teenager. Which store did the best job in serving the customer?

BEGINNING DESIGN PROBLEM

Men's Sportswear

Invent a customer profile for a successful career man in an urban area. It should include the following elements:

Age	Occupation	Residential area
Sports interests	Income range	Height/size
Type of car	Marital status	Taste level

Defining these specifics will provide a life style profile to guide your designs. Create two business suits, remembering that various professions require subtle differences in apparel. For example, a person in auto sales would dress much more casually than a trial lawyer or banker.

Next, design two spectator sportswear outfits for your fictitious customer. Would a man who dresses conservatively for business dress flamboyantly or casually when off the job? One of these outfits should be appropriate for "casual Friday" or business casual wear. Encouraging businessmen to dress less formally was a clever marketing strategy that began with the Levi Strauss Docker's line. Workers in "dot com" (computer) businesses dressed casually and the trend spread to many other occupations.

Illustrate your project and include a profile of your customer and an outline of his life style requirements.

ADVANCED DESIGN PROBLEM

Young Men's Active Wear

Design a group of coordinates for young men interested in surfing or board sports. The base goods for the group is basic white cotton shirting and white poly/cotton jersey or fleece (typically used for T-shirts and sweatshirts.) Base the theme of the group on developing interesting images that are either embroidered or screen-printed on the base goods.

The group should consist of several shorts and two long pants (a basic and a novelty style.) Add a sleeveless tank, a basic T-shirt body, and several novelty sweatshirt tops. Present the design logo and the group in illustration form and critique it as a class activity.

VOCABULARY

Research various men's wear lines and designer names as enrichment vocabulary terms for this chapter.

TEST AND QUIZ QUESTIONS

1. What elements of men's wear were developed during the 1920s? (page 337)

2. Discuss the two basic elements in formal men's wear and how they have influenced each other during the decades of the 1960s through 1980s. (pages 339-341)

3. What is the main trade paper for the men's wear industry? (page 348)

4. Describe how private label merchandise and the retailer as a manufacturer have altered men's wear product development. (page 344)

5. How do designers research men's wear trends? (pages 348-350)

6. Name four popular domestic men's wear magazines. (pages 348-349)

UNIT 4
APPAREL CATEGORIES

CHAPTER 10: TOPS AND COATS

SUPPLEMENTARY TEACHING INFORMATION

As you lecture on the various kinds of bodices, blouses, jackets, and coats, show actual examples from your collection. Use period clothing if you have it available because of the many interesting sleeve treatments and details used in the past.

Demonstrate the fit of sleeves by trying on jackets and blouses using your students as models. Young people often assume that contemporary garments are the only possible styling alternatives. Broaden their experience by showing them photographs of garments with unusual styling details. Analyze the silhouette of each item by darkening your classroom and standing a model in a doorway that has back lighting (from a hall or the outside.) This removes distracting details and the personality of the model from the image of the garment and allows you to discuss the abstract silhouette with your class. Collect and share the following:

Padded shoulder garments -- collect garments from the 1940s and compare them to 1980s garments, especially those designed by Norma Kamali. Demonstrate the built-up shoulder. Measure the depth of the shoulder pad. Investigate the sleeve and discuss how the cut must differ to accommodate a shoulder pad. Compare the styled shoulder pad used in a more conventional jacket to an outrageously large pad. Does removal of the pad alter the drape and silhouette of the jacket or blouse?

The raised shoulder – this higher arm's eye gives a small neat and more youthful look to the entire body. As a styling device, the high shoulder line is most successful on sizes 2 through 12. This shoulder emphasizes a heavy upper arm unless a very full sleeve is added. Courrege garments from the 1960s illustrate this sleeve best.

The drop shoulder – demonstrate this style with a man tailored shirt or other drop shouldered garment. Does this sleeve give the silhouette a youthful look? Does it have an informal appearance?

The kimono – show a kimono sleeve in a classic Japanese kimono and then in western styles in both soft and crisp fabrics. Which is most flattering? What are the plus factors for this sleeve? Go beyond current fashion and consider general fit and flexibility when wearing a kimono sleeve.

The dolman sleeve – try on an exaggerated dolman and analyze the silhouette. Would this style work in a crisp fabric? Compare this to the fitted dolmans typical of Claire

McCardell's styles that had a gusset added to facilitate movement. Discuss styling possibilities.

The raglan sleeve – analyze this silhouette. Discuss its fashion personality and practicality. Compare a classic sweatshirt raglan with more formal styles.

Show the students a man-tailored shirt and discuss the sleeve construction. Show them a constructed sleeve placket and a formal French cuff.

Investigate the back of several kinds of knits and identify the full fashion, intarsia, jacquard, and other knitting techniques. Analyze the "cut" or number of stitches per inch. Distinguish between hand and machine knits fashion sweaters.

FIELD TRIP RECOMMENDATIONS

Coat and Suit Manufacturer

Schedule a trip to a coat and suit manufacturer. Ask the guest lecturer to show their line and discuss how the garments are made. Discuss the fabrics that are used. Wool, the traditional outerwear fabric, is becoming scarce and expensive. Tri-blends, usually woven in Italy, are made of a mixture of wool and other man-made and novelty fibers that duplicate the look of wool at a lower price. What other fabrics are coat and suit manufacturers using instead of wool?

Investigate the fleece market, especially PolarTec, made by Malden Mills, out of recycled plastic bottles. Explore the wide range of artificial fur fabrications and discuss the ramifications of fake fur.

Discuss how old-world tailors are gradually leaving the workforce. How are they being replaced? Are production short cuts being substituted for classic tailoring methods? Are coats being manufactured out of the country where labor costs less? Which countries seem to make the most product? Compare and contrast the construction methods used for men's suits and those used in women's wear.

Shop a Coat and Suit Specialist

Shop several junior coat and suit departments or specialty stores. Analyze the merchandise mix. Pay particular attention to the rainwear. What percentage is foreign made? Where are the coats being manufactured? Compare prices of domestic and foreign items with similar detailing. Evaluate the merchandise based on quality and price of the item. Do the same investigation for leather retailers who specialize in outerwear.

GENERAL FASHION PROBLEMS

Historic Sportswear: Claire McCardell

Study the famous sportswear designer Claire McCardell. Read her excellent book (now out of print) *What Shall I Wear? The What, Where, When and How Much of Fashion* by Claire McCardell (Simon and Schuster, New York, 1956).
Collect McCardell garments. She designed for Townley and Townley Frocks manufactured during the 1940s, 1950s, and early 1960s. Some museums also collect these garments. Discuss the unusual cuts and details that made McCardell garments unique. Discuss Claire McCardell's contributions to the fashions of the period.

Outerwear

Discuss the evolution of outerwear fashions. Traditionally, a woman purchased one "good wool coat" each winter. When did that practice change? The cost of fur coats manufactured off shore has dropped dramatically yet sales of less expensive fur garments have been compromised by animal rights advocates and the fur market has been severely impacted by this movement. Track the politics of wearing fur and how it has affected outerwear.

Leather coats and jackets have become more affordable and fashionable. Many designers include leather garments in their collections. How has this trend affected specialty item lines that manufacture leather outerwear? Discuss the many simulated leather fabrications and how they have changed the market.

Is there a trend toward coat substitutes? Consider how life styles have changed, how climate affects outerwear choices and the compatibility of jackets with changing hemlines.

MERCHANDISING PROBLEM

Prior to the late 1990s, suits were sold in three departments, the coat and suit department, all levels of Designer Sportswear, and the dress department. The traditional suit sold as a unit in the coat and suit department is rare today, though it is still found in high priced designer salons. Occasionally dress departments carry a suit look though these "suits" are costumes (a coat and dress or a jacket and dress) and usually lack the structure and construction details of a tailored jacket. Today, the greatest number of suits are sold in sportswear departments.

Tailored jackets, skirts, pants, and coats are usually made from a heavier weight fabric than accessory blouses and shirts. Soft pieces include blouses, shirts, sweaters, and accessory pieces. Discuss how separates have come to dominate the suit market.

Evaluate the following points:

- Variety of fabrications available for tailored pieces versus accessory pieces
- Price range of a total outfit
- Quality of construction of both tailored and soft pieces
- How fashion influences matched or miss-matched suits
- Fit – bottoms compatible with tops
- Selection of accessory pieces

Compare merchandise from the dress department with true tailored suits. Look for MOB (Mother of the Bride) ensembles and dresses as you shop this department. If you were a customer looking for a suit costing between $300 and $400, where would you purchase it?

BETINNING DESIGN PROBLEMS

Traditional Suit

Design a traditional suit consisting of a jacket, skirt and soft-top. How has the suit changed? Does the jacket have to match the skirt? Shop stores so you know the merchandising options. Design a weekender wardrobe for a working woman, age 25 to 40, who lives in a cool climate. Expand the basic concept of a suit and add flexible pieces that will give the traveling woman two different looks, one for a formal business meeting and a second appropriate for an informal urban tourist. Keep packing to a minimum and consider using accessory pieces to make the basics more versatile. Fabricate, illustrate, and critique.

Budget Suit Group

Design four or five corduroy components that can be combined into a casual suit for the budget category. Select the wale and color of the corduroy. Corduroy is a traditional transitional/fall fabric. Experiment with novelty treatments of the wale. Illustrate and critique.

Coordinates

Assign students to shop missy or junior separates departments that sell tops and blouses to gather information on pricing, fabrication, and general styling trends. An excellent line to investigate is Façonnable. The foundation of this upscale women's casual line is a classic cotton shirt offered in a wide variety of patterns and color stories with basic casual sportswear pieces to accompany the shirts. Owned by Nordstrom, the line is sold in stand-alone stores and departments within Nordstrom.

After researching retail lines, ask the students to design a basic blouse or top concept as well as a group of separates that would compliment the soft pieces. Require them to select a color range for the top fabrics (up to five) that would go with bottom weight colors they have selected. Consider styles in jackets, skirts and pants that are compatible with all the top styles. Sketch, fabricate, and present the group as a class project.

ADVANCED DESIGN PROBLEMS

Bring an example of a fancy blanket to class (like a wonderful Indian blankets woven by Pendleton). Plaid blankets with fringe trims are also appropriate. The blanket should be large enough to accommodate the pieces of a coat pattern.

Ask the students to design an outerwear garment and plan how it would be cut from the blanket to maximize pattern or fringe details. Have them draw the outlines of the pattern pieces on a scaled rectangle that represents the blanket. Encourage the students to eliminate as many seams as possible. Use accent fabrics or leather trims to edge the garment. Review unusual hardware closings.

Clip photographs of designer garments (Bonnie Cashin--a designer who worked in the 1960s and 1970s will provide great examples) as inspiration. Have students sketch and present their blanket layouts for a final critique.

Hand-Knit Sweaters

Assign students a sweater project. Investigate manufactured sweaters that have a hand-knit look. Research yarns available and stitches that can be duplicated on a large cut (stitch) full fashion knitting machine. Use magazines and craft books that focus on knitting for reference material. Knit several swatches to create the knit fabric. Design three bodies using the knit-down swatch and illustrate each. A variety of bodies are typical of a group so include pullovers, turtlenecks, cardigans and novelties. Plan a color story and offer the group in at least two colors.

Students who are able to knit may wish to include novelty stitch treatments like jacquard, intarsia, embroidery, and so forth in their designs. Some students may have experience on knitting machines that produce hand loomed knits and can adapt this project to that type of fabrication.

The most complicated sweaters are made in Europe or the Orient. Domestic mills are clustered in New Jersey, the southern states, and California. Most make simple knits, but innovative sweater fabricators do exist. Seek them out if possible. French Rags, a California firm that makes knit-to-order garments, sells their product through representatives at "in-home" sales parties. A sales representative for this line would make an excellent guest lecturer.

67

TEST AND QUIZ QUESTIONS

1. Describe three ways of shaping fabric to fit the torso. (pages 363-364)

2. What are the two main sleeve structures? (pages 369-376)

3. Diagram a sleeve (page 370) and have students identify the:

Bicep line	Cap
Elbow dart	Underarm seam
Ease notches	Placket line

4. Diagram the following sleeves (pages 375-379) cut in one with the bodice and ask students to name each:

Raglan	Kimono	Gusset dolman
Gusset batwing	Drop bandeau	

5. Describe the classic Channel jacket. (page 383)

6. What are the differences between a cut and sew knit and a full fashion knit?

   (pages 383-386)

7. Define the following knit terms: (pages 388-389)

Intarsia	Jacquard	Hand loomed knit

CHAPTER 11: SKIRTS

SUPPLEMENTARY TEACHING INFORMATION

Lecture and show skirts from your collection.

Discuss skirt lengths. Refer to the evolution of skirt lengths from the mid 1960s to the present. Compare the shapes used during the 1960s with those currently being used. Compare the period when the "mini" was forced on customers before they were ready to accept it and again when the ill-fated "midi" was launched to the boos and hisses of customers. Revolutionary fashion rarely succeeds, but evolution changes the proportion and look of garments over a period of time allowing customers to adjust their expectations and wardrobes gradually. Compare fashion periods when one length is fashionable versus a time period when many different proportions are acceptable. How does skirt length affect the length of jackets and other accessory pieces?

How do pants fit into the hemline question? Are they a substitute when customers are confused about hemline fashions? Do pant hemlines and pant leg width influence proportion? Discuss the various proportions that occur with a variety of skirt lengths.

Ask these questions of your class:

1. Are you confused about skirt lengths currently in fashion?
2. Do you wear both long and short skirts/pants or do you have a preference?
3. Do long skirts signify "evening/formal" wear as they have in the past?
4. Do different occasions demand different skirt lengths?
5. What accessory pieces affect skirt hemlines?
6. When buying a skirt, what fabrications are most fashionable for long and short styles?

MERCHANDISING PROBLEM

Shop a missy department and a junior sportswear department. Compare and contrast the skirts you find in each. Shop the denim section in the junior department. Is the styling in this fabric more advanced or conservative than in other fabrics? Are any categories missing in the skirt department that your students would like to wear? Ask the students to evaluate the quality of the merchandise compared to the price.

BEGINNING DESIGN PROBLEM

Design a skirt line for a sophisticated junior separates line for fall. Use the following fabric groups and style three to four garments for each group:

    1. Corduroy   2. Stone washed denim   3. Wool flannel

ADVANCED DESIGN PROBLEM

Design a group of three skirts that do not use zippers or buttons as fasteners. Consider wraps, ties, sashes and so forth to secure the fabric. Study ethnic costumes from India, Central America (look at men's costumes too) and the Orient for inspiration.

TEST AND QUIZ QUESTIONS

1. Name the four basic skirt silhouettes. (pages 395-396)

2. What are the common ways to shape a dirndl or a straight skirt? (pages 396-397)

3. Name and sketch or describe three pleats commonly used in pleated skirts. (page 399)

4. Why are circular skirts so costly and impractical to make? (pages 402-403)

5. Describe or sketch and name 6 skirt lengths. (pages 405-406)

CHAPTER 12: DRESSES

SUPPLEMENTAL TEACHING INFORMATION

Show the students examples of dresses relevant to the lecture from your collection of garments.

Discuss the role of the dress in current fashion. The dress has become less important as women opt for the comfort, versatility, and fashion appeal of pants and casual sportswear. Prior to 1940, women wore skirts and dresses most of the time. Currently, various hemlines are in fashion and customers have a great variety of silhouettes and options, but the versatility of mix and match sportswear continues to attract many customers. On the other hand, a dress offers the customer a total look without the problem of coordinating separates. A dress is feminine and usually less expensive than a collection of separates.

Discuss when and why some people prefer to wear a dress. Check recent issues of *Women's Wear Daily* and other trade papers for their analysis of the dress business. Compare trade reports with consumer magazines like *In Style* to understand the pull publicity has on popular fashion. Compare the demand for dresses in the junior area to those in other dress departments for more mature customers. Discuss the current hot designers and popular lines in the dress area.

GENERAL FASHION PROBLEM

The designer dress department is the source of many inspirational trends and styling themes. Designers who are carried in this department are often the "stars" of fashion and newspapers and magazines review their collections. It is important for design students to recognize the names and fashion personalities of these designers.

Unfortunately it is often difficult for a young student to penetrate the "back room" and the aloof sales people who typically work in a designer dress department. Arrange a field trip to a designer dress department (also called the "salon" in many upscale stores). Ask the buyer or manager to select a time when (s)he is able to discuss the merchandise with students. Focus on the most popular designers, best apparel classifications, and how to approach the wealthy customer. What special selling techniques are used for this customer?

After the field trip, ask students to evaluate the merchandise. Can they relate to it? Ask them to list the names of the designers they remember or take notes during the presentation. Reinforce the "roll call" of famous designers by making display boards with photographs of the designer and a collage of their styles. This material can also be covered with a quiz.

MERCHANDISING PROBLEM

Shop any two of the following kinds of dress departments and evaluate the merchandise based on the following criteria:

1. price range
2. fabrications
3. fashion and basic color stories
4. kinds of prints
5. age range of typical customers
6. types of bodies
7. fit
8. range of classifications (two piece, jump suits, cocktail or dance dresses, etc.)

Compare any two categories:

- budget missy dresses and budget junior dresses
- chain store missy dresses and moderate missy dresses
- moderate junior versus moderate missy dresses
- designer dresses versus bridge designer garments
- contemporary dresses and after five dance dresses

BEGINNING DESIGN PROBLEMS

1. Design a junior occasion group of three dresses with the following specifications:

Season:	spring/summer
Price Range:	moderate
Fabrication:	light weight cottons, prints, rayon, eyelet, and other novelties
Occasion:	graduation dresses, sweet-16 parties, quinceañera (coming out parties for Hispanic girls at 15 years of age) informal weddings and afternoon parties

2. Design junior occasion dress group of three bodies with the following specs:

Season:	holiday
Price Range:	better
Fabrication:	shiny knits, jersey, slinky fabrics, taffeta, crepe back satin and other dressy looks
Occasion:	a youthful but sophisticated look for parties, proms, or dance clubs

Bridal Dress

Using empire costume as inspiration, ask your students to design a wedding dress for a young bride. She has an average, size 9/10 figure. Bring appropriate fabrications to class and show students slides of garments from the Empire Period. If these are not available, many excellent costume history books picture garments from the period (roughly 1795-1820 – especially in the French court of Napoleon). You may also require Internet research on the period. Ask students to select fabrics similar to those of the period. Illustrate the gown and critique.

ADVANCED DESIGN PROBLEMS

The two most important months for weddings are June and December. Ask the students to research wedding dresses by shopping department and specialty stores that sell wedding gowns, reading bride magazines, researching celebrity weddings and period fashions that could be adapted to wedding gowns.

Discuss the changing customs in weddings. Consider the many settings used for weddings (gardens, parks, the beach – even on horseback!). Design wedding and bridesmaid dresses for the following customers/occasions:

June Wedding

A casual wedding at home in a garden with an informal reception that will follow the ceremony. The floral theme is daisies and wild flowers. The pride is active and athletic, age 22 and wears a size 14 dress and is 5' 3" tall. She has blond hair. Consider the figure limitations of this bride and design a garment that will make her look taller and more slender.

December Wedding

A formal winter wedding will be held at a large and rather dark church with a country club reception following. Floral arrangements include red carnations and white roses. The bride is 5'8" tall and wears a size 8 top and a size 12 skirt. She has dark hair and hazel eyes. The bridegroom is nearly 5'9" tall, and the bride would like to minimize her height and stature so they are visually the same height during the ceremony and in the photographs.

Fabricate the dresses thinking of the personality of the bride, the season, and the formality of the ceremony. Illustrate and present for a critique.

(Note: you may wish to ask the students to design a wedding dress for one of their classmates who is planning a wedding. Substitute her figure type and wedding plans for those above.)

TEST AND QUIZ QUESTIONS

1. Compare and contrast the junior and contemporary dress customer. (pages 411-414)

2. Describe a MOB dress. (page 415)

3. What types of specialty dress categories exist? (pages 416-418)

4. Identify the following horizontal divisions of a dress: (page 419)

Low torso	Natural waist	High waist
Empire	Shoulder yoke	

5. Provide examples of a variety of dress bodies and ask the students to identify them. (pages 420-423)

CHAPTER 13: SPORTSWEAR AND PANTS

SUPPLEMENTAL TEACHING INFORMATION

Pants

Discuss pant styling. Ask your students to evaluate their pant wardrobes. Do a count of the kinds, color, and style of their pants. There are two main kinds of traditional pants:

1. the jean fit – very slim or tailored
2. the trouser fit – straight leg and pleated or slim-front torso

Plus, there are many additional fashion silhouettes:

3. hose/tights
4. baggy styles, soft pants
5. shorts
6. peddle pushers and shorter-than-ankle length novelties
7. novelty pants like harem, palazzo, and so forth

Discuss how life styles have changed to allow women to wear pants in many situations. Discuss cultures (China, India, and the Middle East) that have societies that dictate that women wear pants. Ask the students why pants have been the symbol of masculinity in western consumer apparel. Consider the saying, "the one who wears the pants in the family."

Are there any limits to where women can wear pants today? What about religions limitations?

Ask the students to evaluate pant styling. Currently high fashion pant styling emphasizes variety of fit. Jeans have both slim and baggy styling. Contrast this with the popularity of tights and leggings. Discuss how various silhouettes influence the accessories worn with pants.

Discuss researching trends in denim sportswear. Ask students to shop a jeans store investigating high fashion resources and comparing them with the basic jeans makers. Compare and contrast the "cowboy chic" of Wrangler with the slim and baggy silhouettes available from Levi, Guess? and other denim specialists.

Swimwear

Swimwear is a unique market with specialized fabrications, design seasons and styling problems. Track the history of swimwear during the past century using the historic styling illustrations as a guide with your students.

Shop retail catalogs and stores that feature swimwear, and identify makers who are concerned with the fashion picture and those whose niche is athletic competition. Visit the Speedo web site and investigate new fabrications being developed to enhance the speed and performance of swimmers and divers. Compare and contrast the styling of these two markets and the crossover influence each has on the other.

Explore color stories and fabric prints that are popular at a variety of different price points. Compare and contrast junior swimwear to missy lines. Match current fashion in bodies to how the styling affects figure problems.

GENERAL FASHION PROBLEM

Plan a trip or a shopping survey of the contemporary sportswear department. Just as the designer dress department sells the "big names" in missy dress fashions, contemporary and designer sportswear departments carry specific high fashion designers. If possible, visit stand-alone designer sportswear stores like Ralph Lauren, Donna Karen, or Tommy Hilfiger and note the various price points of the popular and designer portions of the collections. Compare the merchandise found in a designer's boutique with that sold in a department store.

Pre-shop departments and alert students to names of designers to look for. If visiting as a group, ask the buyer or manager to discuss leading designers and new fashion trends. Have the students sketch innovative styles so they can remember them after the visit. Ask students to select three favorite items and list the reasons they liked them.

Prepare designer boards as you did with the dress area. A picture of the designer surrounded by his/her styles helps your students remember the names and personalities of each. Quiz students on this material.

MERCHANDISING PROBLEM

Refer to the merchandising problem outlined in Chapter 10 because it is relevant to coats and suits sold in sportswear departments and is also a fit for sportswear.

Have students research a designer sportswear department. Review current lines and research the look and personality of the following designers:

- *Anne Klein and Anne Klein II* -- a designer label and a better sportswear line using some of the same styles a season later
- *Donna Karen and DKNY* – again, the sophisticated expensive line is contrasted with a less expensive, casual companion line
- *Ellen Tracy and E Company* – bridge sportswear designer with a career and casual division
- *Ralph Lauren and Polo and the Lauren Sportswear* – designer sportswear and upscale casual lines; also check out Polo Jeans

- *Tommy Hilfiger* – sportswear for men and women
- *Calvin Klein* – several divisions including high priced sportswear and more casual lines
- *Liz Claiborne* – a popular, better sportswear look

Compare these lines to foreign designer lines like *Escada, Krizia, Armani, Gucci,* and others. Look for common fabrications, silhouettes, themes, and colors.

BEGINNING DESIGN PROBLEM

Have students design a denim line of eight to ten pants and three to four jackets. Use standard 11-ounce indigo denim – either pre-washed or unwashed. Add trims and details that are practical for mass production.

Have students research the conventional jeans departments and measure the width of pant legs and the length of the inseam of five or six popular manufacturer's hot styles. Shop innovative foreign jeans manufacturers for hints on new trends. List the names and sketch the best styles of four or five of the top manufacturers and note the price.

Ask students to look at the *Rockies* pant line carried in western stores. These styled denims are offered in a wide range of colors and feature innovative cuts and details. Many are extremely flattering to a range of figures. Compare these to styles found in trendy lines.

Have students sketch a group and critique it in class.

ADVANCED DESIGN PROBLEMS

Sportswear

Assign students a designer sportswear group to design for fall. Research colors for the season. Refer to the color insert pages for guidance. Integrate the information on organizing a group line and fabrications. Sketch at least 20 different jackets in small thumbnail sketches and review with your instructor. Invite a buyer or guest designer to review the projects at this point. Ask for comments on the color story, fabrications, and preliminary sketches to select the most promising directions.

Students should balance the novelty jackets with a variety of pants, skirts and accessory pieces. Develop the entire line, illustrate and present with appropriate fabrications and colors. Critique as a class project.

Swimwear

Have student design two groups of swimwear, one that features solid fabrics and some type of trim and the second, a print fabric. Develop each group in three bodies using the theme or print consistently throughout the group. Design a print in two color-ways for one group.

Illustrate the groups and include colors and trim for the solid fabrication and a painted croquis of the prints. Critique as a class project.

TEST AND QUIZ QUESTIONS

1. What is the difference between active and spectator sportswear? (page 425)

2. Describe two early pant styles worn by women. (pages 426-427)

3. Who was "Rosie the Riveter" and why was she important to the history of women's pants? (page 428)

4. Describe the origin of the word "denim." (pages 428-429)

5. Name various pant lengths. (page 434)

6. What is the difference between separates and coordinates? (page 435-437)

7. Describe swimwear seasons. (page 447-450)

8. What is the most popular swimwear fabrication today? (page 443-445)

APPENDIX

Apparel manufacturing contributed nearly $9 billion to the Southern California regional economy and represented the largest discrete manufacturing sector in Los Angeles County in 2000. The industry directly employed about 100,000 workers in the region. Many economic pressures caused the west coast industry to dramatically evolve during the first years of the new century. Regional changes mirrored pressures the national industry experienced.

Based on the critical positioning of the Southern California apparel industry as a major economic force in the region, apparel manufacturing was targeted as one of four industries to be analyzed by the Los Angeles Regional Workforce Preparation and Economic Development Collaborative. The report was published by the Community Development Technologies Center, a regional nonprofit organization providing training, applied research, and technical assistance services in community economic development. CDTech was project director for the Los Angeles Regional Workforce Preparation and Economic Development Collaborative.

Many public and private entities participated in the research and report preparation under the direction of editor and project director, Linda Wong. Portions of the report relevant to the national industry are included in the appendix as readings with the hope that they will provide detailed information for fashion design and merchandising instructors that illustrating the compelling forces that are affecting apparel manufacturing and retailing in the United States.

For additional information about the project and the report, *Fashion Forward, Assessing the Future of Apparel Manufacturing in Los Angeles County,* contact:

> Linda J. Wong, Project Director
> Community Development Technologies Center
> 520 West Twenty Third Street
> Los Angeles, California   90007
>> 213-763-2520
>> lwong@pacbell.net

Internet Products available on:

www.laworkforce.org

FASHION FORWARD:
Assessing the Future of
Apparel Manufacturing in Los Angeles County

Industry Trends

The apparel industry is undergoing a dramatic transformation from a manufacturer-driven mass production model to a retailer-driven "quick response" flexible manufacturing model. The past decade was full of innovations in apparel manufacturing, marketing and retailing. The 1990's saw waves of consolidations, signing and implementation of international trade agreements, major shifts in production and retailing processes, introduction of new production technologies, and the rise of e-commerce. These major trends will impact the industry, both nationally and locally, for years to come. A few key trends warrant special consideration. These include the consolidation of the apparel retail sector, the growing importance of branding and private label manufacturing, the rise of licensing, and changes in technology.

Retail Consolidation

The consolidation of apparel retailers is one of the most far-reaching changes to occur in the apparel industry in recent history. Before 1980, retailers were concerned with the wholesale price and the related retail-selling price. Then as the 1980's saw the rise of the discounters, the retail sector started experiencing fierce price competition and retail overcapacity, resulting in substantial losses. Retailers sought to strengthen their positions through mergers and acquisitions, leaving the more vulnerable in a wake of bankruptcies and closures. Susceptibility to bankruptcy and closure would then generate the next round of mergers and acquisitions, a consolidation scenario that has continued into the present.

Figure 2-1: Retail Industry Consolidation Flow Chart

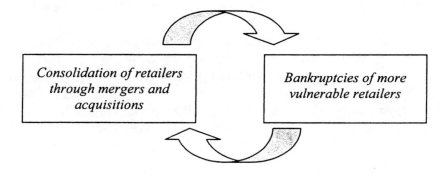

Those retailers still in operation have been forced to re-examine their methods of doing business. Retailers have hired production people to ascertain the actual cost of manufacturing individual items. Improvements in information technology have allowed retailers to track the performance of specific garments and the overall success or failure of particular buyers. Performance tracking has led to smaller individual orders for manufacturers and demands for shorter lead times. A shift has thus occurred from a manufacturing-led to a retailer-driven industry.[22]

Prior to the 1980's, big production runs, long turnaround times, and stock-heavy retail stores characterized the apparel industry. Over the past decade, however, retailers have forced manufacturers to increase the quality of their apparel products, to lower costs and prices, and to deliver smaller volumes of retail-ready goods in a "just-in-time" environment (short and frequent production runs).

Apparel industry experts suggest that this transformation began in the mid-1980's when J.C. Penney decided to raise its quality standards for clothing.[23] J.C. Penney had found that their goods were overpriced and that they lost large sums of money when stock did not sell as anticipated. Penney's had exacerbated the situation by sticking to its merchandising formula, buying only at the beginning of a season and not reordering those items that were strong sellers.

"Quick response" became one solution to this problem. This strategy for implementing just-in-time production is not limited to fashion-sensitive or trendy apparel—it has been adopted by most apparel retailers since consumers are much less willing to buy in advance of a season. Today, it can take as little as one week from design to rack for commodity items.[24] Inventory levels have reached new lows, as retailers refuse to carry any inventory longer than 60 days. By December 1999, apparel retailers' inventory-to-sales ratio had reached 1.30,[25] an indication that manufacturing processes have become more efficient.

Retailers also use "charge-backs" to reduce their inventory costs. "Charge-backs" are an arrangement whereby a percentage of the cost of unsold product is billed back to the manufacturer; the product itself may or may not be returned. Any "charge-back" provisions and terms are part of the purchase order. Similar terms may also apply to any promotional costs associated with "charge-back" product; that is, the manufacturer may have to assume a greater share of any joint ("co-op") advertising dollars spent featuring the product. Retailers are using the "charge-back" mechanism more frequently to recoup the costs of poorly selling items, shipping or tagging errors, etc.—again, shifting more of the risk to the manufacturers. To quote an anonymous industry insider, "Retail charge-back centers have become profit centers."

However, retailers themselves are experiencing a profit squeeze from the consumer. The apparel industry as a whole is still under pricing pressures from intense competition and the inability to raise prices. In fact, in constant dollar terms, the price of clothing has actually declined over the past ten years. Consumers have become much more value-sensitive, and the widespread practice of constant markdowns and promotional sales and the increased prevalence of discounters and outlets have conditioned the consumer to never pay full price. Today, customers use sale prices

---

[22] Larry Jacobs, "The Genie is out of the Bottle! A Comprehensive Analysis of the Current State of our Industry," *California Apparel News*, 26 June 1998.
[23] Interview with Bruce Berton, CPA, Stonefield Josephson, Inc, 12 July 2001.
[24] *Ibid.*
[25] "Industry Report: Apparel & Footwear Industry, *US Business Reporter* [magazine on-line]; available from *http://www.usbrn.com*, Internet; accessed 13 February 2002.

as benchmarks for every-day purchases. This leaves retailers and manufacturers little price flexibility to pass on costs to consumers.[26]

Retail's Changing Landscape

In a further effort to reduce costs and increase profitability, retailers began merging and consolidating at a fast pace in the 1980's. In the process, several thousand retailers have gone bankrupt. As discount stores' share of the retail market has increased, the number of companies operating in this market segment has been drastically reduced. Wal-Mart and Target have been the ascending stars. Regional discounters have felt more competitive pressure than ever as Wal-Mart opens more "Supercenters," and Target and K-Mart expanded nationally.[27]

Already the top 20 retailers account for upward of 90 percent of all apparel sold in the U.S.[28] Wal-Mart, with the lowest administrative cost ratio in the industry, is the largest retailer in the world, as measured by sales. Wal-Mart continues to distance itself from the rest of the pack, thanks in part to its growth in international sales. Worldwide, the company's revenues were more than $191 billion for the fiscal year ended January 31, 2001. Earnings were approximately $6.3 billion—or higher than the sales of all but the 36 largest retailers on the Top 100 chart of Stores On-Line. Headed by Wal-Mart, the 10 largest retailers accounted for sales of $536 billion, or about 53 percent of the top 100 retailers' aggregate volume of just over $1 trillion. The top 100 total for the year 2000 represented an 11 percent increase over 1999, when the 100 largest retailers had total sales of $963 billion.[29] Indeed, the retail market has become dominated by just a handful of mammoth corporations.

The Department Stores[30]

While the nation's largest retailers have grown larger, considerable consolidation has occurred among mid-level companies. Mid-level chains such as Montgomery Ward have been caught between off-price retailers and discounters on one end and high-end department stores on the other. Chicago-based Montgomery Ward Inc. operated under bankruptcy protection for several years. Montgomery Ward Inc. and Massachusetts-based Bradlees Inc., two retail chains that together operated approximately 356 stores, filed for bankruptcy in December 2000.

The bankruptcies created a flood of new retail real estate coming into the market as Ward sold the 100 stores it owned outright. Saks Inc., Dillard's and May Company have all purchased a number of former Ward stores. Ward rented its remaining 152 stores and Bradlees rented all of

---

[26] "Industry Analysis," *US Business Reporter* [magazine on-line], 18 August 2000; available from *http://www.activemediaguide. index.htm*; Internet.

[27] David P. Schulz, "The Nation's Biggest Retail Companies," *Stores Magazine* [magazine on-line], July 1998, available from *http://www.stores.org/archives/july98cover.html*; Internet.

[28] Berton interview, 12 July 2001.

[29] Shultz, "The Nation's Biggest Retail Companies."

[30] The term "department store" technically refers to stores like Macy's and Sears that also sell "hard goods" such as furniture and appliances. However, the majority of department store revenues come from "soft goods," i.e. apparel. Because department stores compete for apparel sales with other large specialty retailers such as Saks Fifth Avenue or Nordstrom, the public tends to lump both department stores and larger apparel specialty retailers together in the "department store" category. For discussion purposes, both groups have been included in this section.

its 105 stores. Termination of the leases for these 257 stores made more retail space available for other department stores, specialty stores, and discounters.

Another result of the two bankruptcies was a deluge of discounted merchandise as both chains liquidated their inventories, further depressing overall retail prices. The two bankruptcies may trigger a second wave of consolidation in the retail industry, according to various analysts, particularly if the U.S. economy continues to slow and other weakened chains succumb to the predicted tougher times ahead.[31]

Consolidation has fundamentally reshaped the department store segment over the past decade. Through mergers and acquisitions—which are less costly than expansions—department stores have aimed to increase their strength and fend off discount stores and specialty stores that continue to eat away at their market share. During the 1980's, department stores were the object of takeovers and leveraged buy-outs, resulting in a wave of bankruptcies and closings. These events, plus several major mergers and consolidations, reduced the number of major department stores in the industry from eleven with total sales of approximately $30 billion in 1984, to two major department store groups in 2001--Federated Department Stores and May Company. Including their two main competitors, the four top department stores today account for nearly $50 billion in total sales.[32] Although dwarfed by Wal-Mart and encroached upon by other major discounters and specialty stores, the department stores are major historical references and remain central economic powerhouses within the apparel industry.

Federated's and May's main competitors are the younger Saks Inc. and Dillard's. It should be noted that Saks Inc. and Dillard's were quicker to adopt new technologies than Federated and May. Appendix A provides a chronology of consolidations among the top four department stores. It reveals the myriad of bankruptcies, mergers and acquisitions that have taken place and shows an increased rate of consolidation since the 1980's. The following paragraphs describe each department store company in greater detail.

Federated Department Stores, based in Cincinnati and New York, is the nation's largest department store retailer, with annual sales of more than $18 billion and 450 stores in 34 states, Puerto Rico, and Guam. In addition to its Bloomingdale's and Macy's chains, Federated runs five regional chains: Lazarus, The Bon Marché, Burdines, Rich's, and Goldsmith's. Federated is focusing increasingly on direct retailing. In addition to its catalogs (Macy's by Mail and Bloomingdale's by Mail), it sells through the Internet (macys.com, bloomingdales.com) and has an interest in online registry provider WeddingChannel.com. Federated is now selling its catalog and Internet marketer, Fingerhut Companies. Fingerhut Companies, Inc. is the second largest consumer catalog company in the U.S., and sells a broad range of products and services directly to consumers through catalogs, direct marketing and the Internet.

May Company, with approximately $14.5 billion in sales, is the second largest department store operator in the U.S. behind Federated. May currently has 425 stores coast-to-coast under a dozen names: Lord & Taylor, Foley's, Filene's, Hecht's, Strawbridge's, Robinsons-May, Famous-

---

[31] Louis Chunovic, "Bankruptcies at Bradlees, Ward's Resonate in Retail," *ApparelNews.Net* [magazine on-line], 10-16 August 2001, available from *http://ApparelNews.Net*; Internet

[32] "Overview: The Department Store Industry," National Center for the Workplace, prepared by The Institute of Industrial Relations (Berkeley, CA: University of California 1996); Stores On-Line, *Top 100 Retailers.*

Barr, L.S. Ayres, Meier & Frank, The Jones Store, and Kaufmann's. The company primarily sells branded apparel, shoes, cosmetics, and home furnishings to middle- and upper-middle income buyers. May is striving to reach out to younger customers with hip brands. In 2000 the company expanded into the matrimonial market with its purchase of 120-chain store David's Bridal.

Dillard's is now the third largest U.S. department store operator, with about 340 locations in 30 states and annual sales of more than $8.7 billion. The company's acquisition of Mercantile Stores in 1998 boosted its presence in the Midwest and South; it has also been acquiring other stores in the Midwest and West in recent years. Dillard's caters to a middle- to upper-middle-income clientele, selling name brand and private label merchandise, with an emphasis on clothing and home furnishings. Women's and juniors' clothing account for nearly a third of sales. Dillard's also operates a small-event ticket sales chain in the Southwest. The Dillard family runs the organization and elects most of its directors. Because it is a privately held company, detailed information on its acquisitions is not readily available.

Saks Incorporated, formerly Proffitt's, is the fourth largest U.S. department store operator, with annual sales of nearly $6.6 billion and about 350 stores in 40 states. Concentrated in the Southeast and Midwest, Saks Inc.'s Department Store Group (DSG) consists of the following regional chains: Parisian, Younkers, Carson Pirie Scott, McRae's, Proffitt's, Herberger's, Boston Store, and Bergner's. Saks Inc. also operates Saks Fifth Avenue Enterprises, which includes 62 Saks Fifth Ave. stores, 49 Saks Off 5th outlet stores, and Saks Direct, which runs two catalog operations--Folio and Bullock & Jones--and saks.com. The company acquired luxury retailer Saks Holdings in 1998. Saks had intended to spin off Saks Fifth Avenue, Saks Direct (catalog and Internet operations), and Saks Off 5th as a separate public company; however, it scrapped this plan, citing poor conditions in the luxury retail market.[33]

Retail Consolidation Impacts Apparel Manufacturers

Bankruptcies and consolidations of retail organizations have caused bankruptcies and consolidations downstream, and it appears that this trend is continuing. With the closure and consolidation of smaller retail stores and divisions, administrative functions have been centralized, and chain-wide systems have been created. Apparel merchandising–where the purchasing of apparel products takes place–has become tightly consolidated and has resulted in fewer buyers in search of apparel. Federated, May, and Dillard's have been at the forefront of instituting this vendor intensification.[34]

Fewer unique retailers buying apparel for their stores means that a greater share of apparel orders is concentrated among a smaller number of apparel manufacturers. To survive, apparel manufacturers not only have to be price competitive and maintain low overheads; increasingly, they also need to have mechanized operations and use information systems that are compatible with the retailers. Electronic Data Interchange (EDI), the computer technology that directly connects retailers and manufacturers, can make or break large apparel manufacturers today.

---

[33] Hoovers Company Capsules, Company Websites [report on-line]; available from *http://www.hoovers.com*; Internet.
[34] "Overview: The Department Store Industry."

As retailers continue to push for shorter lead times on seasonal merchandise, to demand faster reorders of fast selling items, and to expect manufacturers to hold down prices and to adopt EDI systems, small manufacturers (i.e., those with revenues under $10 million) find it increasingly difficult to remain profitable and competitive. Apparel manufacturers complain that the prices they receive for goods have not increased in over a decade, despite several increases in the minimum wage and the rising costs of other inputs.[35] Many manufacturers are simply being squeezed out of this supply chain.

Some are managing to stay afloat by adapting creatively to the new business environment. For example, in June 2001, Harkham Industries, which includes the Jonathan Martin and Hype labels, announced a joint venture with Los Angeles-based Swat/Fame for Jonathan Martin junior apparel, sportswear and dresses. The joint venture with Swat/Fame is one of several planned joint ventures for Harkham Industries.[36] Other smaller apparel manufacturers have simply met their demise—in 2001, the obituaries included Los Angeles's Chorus Line, Carole Little and Bugle Boy. In spite of this, new designers are continually setting up shop, and there continues to be a proliferation of manufacturers at the bottom. However, the life span at the bottom is much shorter than at the top, and this phenomenon is becoming more pronounced.[37]

Branding, Private Labeling, and Licensing

Branding, private labeling, and licensing of apparel all reflect the key role that branding plays in selling apparel to consumers.

Branding

Branding, or the establishment of name recognition and the development of customer loyalty, is the key to success for those apparel firms wanting to do business with major retailers. Branding is the ultimate concern of designers and manufacturers, and increasingly apparel retailers. Without a brand name, consumers can only judge each individual garment on the basis of its merits. A consumer may think, "These jeans look good, and they fit well, but I've never heard of this brand before. Will they hold up as well as Levi's? Since I know Levi's will last forever, maybe I should just get those, even if they cost a little more."

This hypothetical train of thought illustrates another important facet of branding—reputation. People buy Samsonite luggage, Columbia Sportswear, Levi's jeans, and Speedo swimwear not only because they look good, but also because they perform well over time. These brands have achieved a reputation for durability, consistent performance, and value for their cost. Other manufacturers may seek a reputation for cutting-edge fashion. Young women expect cutting-edge designs and fabric from Bebe or BCBG, which is the basis for their reputation.

---

[35] Bonacich and Appelbaum, *Behind the Label*.
[36] Darryl James, "Harkham, Swat/Fame Form Joint Venture for Jonathan Martin Label, *ApparelNews.Net* [magazine on-line], 27 June 2001, available from *http://ApparelNews.net*; Internet.
[37] Phone Interview with Judi Kessler, 10 July 2001.

Today, capturing customer loyalty is what makes or breaks an apparel business because it provides assurance that a certain segment of the consumer market will regularly purchase the brand. A brand, once developed, helps to reduce apparel manufacturers' risk by creating consistent sales. Because profit margins are so slim for lesser-known manufacturers, and the risk associated with developing new apparel lines each fashion season is so high, the development of a brand name that will yield consistent sales is an apparel firm's ticket to success.

In the fashion industry, branding applies to more than just apparel; it seeks to shape the "lifestyle" of its customers by creating a mood or image and using it to market a variety of products from jeans to watches to perfume to handbags. Tommy Hilfiger, for example, in addition to its original line of casual wear, has branded its own lines of men's and women's outerwear, shoes, perfume, and accessories. Ralph Lauren has gone so far as to develop its own line of household paint. "Lifestyle branding" seeks to reach nearly every aspect of a consumer's life. Once a brand is developed, the company must develop its products carefully and consistently to retain customer loyalty and remain successful.

One of the key principles of developing and maintaining a brand name is consistency, or sticking with one consumer market niche: high-end, mid-range or discount. If a manufacturer originally sells its apparel to high-end stores and then begins selling its products to off-price retailers and discounters, it has excluded itself from ever being able to sell that brand to the high-end department and specialty stores again. If customers who regularly buy a particular brand name detect a decline in quality or unwanted changes in the style of the brand, consumer loyalty may evaporate. The case of Mossimo, discussed below, bears witness to the difficulty manufacturers face in developing and maintaining their brands.

However, in certain consumer market segments fashion remains fickle, especially among juniors and girls. These consumers tend to remain loyal to certain brands for only so long. Today, what is fashionable for them is "discovering" new and unique brands, not donning established labels. Without a doubt, new independent designers are the real trend in juniors and girls fashion.[38]

Private Labeling

Major retailers are increasingly jumping onto the branding bandwagon, eliminating their traditional apparel suppliers and developing product lines directly through private label programs. Macy's boasts one of the largest retail private label programs in its Inc. brand, second in volume only to J.C. Penney's Arizona label. The GAP, Banana Republic and Old Navy are among the most visible private label retailers, although almost all retailers now are developing private labels of their own. According to Bobbin Magazine, 35 percent of all 1999 women's wear sales were under retailers' private label brands.[39]

Retailers began developing the concept of private label merchandising in the 1980's as a cost saving strategy, essentially eliminating the branded manufacturer. In the production of private labels, retailers know the exact cost of manufacturing, and retailers predetermine the amount of gross profit they will allow their manufacturers. For branded merchandise, the manufacturer has

---

[38] Interview with the CFO of a local design firm who wishes to remain anonymous, 1 July 2001.
[39] Kathleen DesMarteau, "Year in Review: Defining the Key Issues of 1999," *Bobbin Magazine*, December 1999.

greater say than the retailer in determining the price the retailer must pay to acquire branded apparel. With traditional retail, the balance of power rests more evenly between the branded manufacturer and the apparel retailer because, in order for the retailer to do well, the retailer must carry the most popular brand names. With the retailer developing its own brand names (private label manufacturing), the retailer tips the balance of power in its favor because it is the retailer who directly determines the price.

From the perspective of apparel manufacturers, private label work is considered the "bread and butter" of many smaller designer/manufacturers. By coupling private label and multiple label garment production with the production of their own brands, they can reduce their risk and increase their stability.

Tarrant Apparel Group, based in Los Angeles, is the largest private label manufacturer in Southern California, with $395 million in net sales in the year 2000. The company's specialty is women's jeans, but it also offers moderately priced casual wear, all under retail store labels. It serves specialty retailers, mass merchants, national department stores and branded wholesalers by designing, merchandising, and contracting for the manufacture of casual, moderately-priced apparel for women, men and children. It has a vast and complex web of operations globally and has acquired companies all over the United States, as well as in Mexico and Asia. Contractors in China and Latin America make most of the company's products, but it has become more vertically integrated by purchasing manufacturing plants in Mexico. Tarrant Apparel expanded its women's lines with the purchase of a 51 percent stake in Needletex, owner of the Jane Doe brand of women's sportswear. It also bought CMG, which makes J.C. Penney's Arizona label. The Limited's chain accounts for nearly 45 percent of sales. Tarrant's other major clients include Lane Bryant, Lerner New York, K-Mart and Target. [40]

Licensing Agreements

Like private labeling, licensing emerged in the apparel industry as a response to the increased importance of branding. Once an apparel manufacturer has developed a strong brand name and years of loyalty, the company may decide to shed its manufacturing operations and make money by selling the brand name itself. In license agreements, apparel manufacturers sell the right to use their brand names on garments or other products they produce. In some cases, the branded apparel manufacturer may continue producing its own clothing line, but may license its name to a company that manufactures handbags, or watches, or shoes. In this manner, the branded apparel manufacturer can make a profit from "lifestyle" branding through licensing, while continuing to focus on apparel manufacturing.

Licensing is becoming increasingly popular, and designers may license multiple manufacturers simultaneously. This practice allows companies to expand into new markets without additional capital commitments for warehousing, offices, personnel or inventory. Licensing is especially prevalent in the case of brand name accessories such as watches, shoes, and other products whose production is distinctly different from apparel.

---

[40] Hoovers Company Capsules, Company Websites [report on-line] available from *http://www.hoovers.com/co/capsule/5/0,2163,44025,00.html.*

In addition, designers who license their own brands may simultaneously produce private label merchandise for other companies. Licensing arrangements are generally beneficial for all parties involved. This practice allows the licensee to take advantage of a well-known brand name, though generating less profit than it would with its own brand, while it gives the licensor a less costly method of taking its products to new markets.[41]

Licensing is essentially a business agreement between designers, manufacturers and distributors. While each licensing agreement is different, common arrangements provide for a three- to ten-year duration, often with renewal options, and provide for either royalties as a percentage of net sales or for minimum royalty payments. Licensing agreements are often granted only for a particular product group or market and usually give the licensor ultimate control over the product design and quality.

The licensing process itself takes various forms. It can be very "hands-on" or very "hands-off" in terms of the designer's role, ranging from the designer simply receiving a percentage of the licensee's total profits on the sale with minimum oversight, to the designer being in close contact with the licensee throughout the production process. The licensing agreement can require the designer's approval on everything from cutting, sewing, and dyeing, to distribution.[42]

The continued value of a brand is dependent upon ensuring a high quality standard for the product, which often requires extensive monitoring of the licensees. Foreign licensees make monitoring more difficult, and lack of proximity can compound any problems with timeliness or quality control. If monitoring is lax and quality standards drop, the brand will become associated with inferior products and will cease to have consumer loyalty, resulting in the company's market devaluation. For example, when Calvin Klein put his company on the market in 1999, it did not sell because potential buyers feared the far-flung network of licensees who manufacture its products—despite the fact that the Calvin Klein licensing network makes about $5 billion a year through licensing alone.

Case Study: Mossimo Inc.

Founded in 1987 in Irvine, California, Mossimo Inc. is a designer of men's, women's, boys' and girls' active-wear apparel and footwear; home textiles; cosmetics; eyewear and other fashion accessories such as jewelry, watches, handbags, and belts; and hair care products. Mossimo was also a manufacturer and a private label distributor.[43] Five years ago the business was booming and the company went public; two years ago the company nearly went bankrupt. Mossimo grew too fast. In 2001, the company laid off 90 percent of its workforce (approximately 300 employees), closed its two boutiques in Costa Mesa and Ontario and its showrooms across the country, and entered into a three-year, $28 million plus royalties license agreement with Minneapolis-based Target Corporation.[44]

---

[41] Jordan K. Speer, "Top Fifty: Apparel Manufacturers Take on a New Face," *Bobbin Magazine*, June 2001.
[42] Anonymous interview.
[43] "Mossimo, Inc. Reports Fourth Quarter and Fiscal Year 2000 Results," *Business Wire*, 17 April 2001.
[44] Leslie Earnest, "Mossimo to Fire 90% of Workers, Close Stores," *Los Angeles Times*, Orange Country Edition, Business Section, 16 May 2000; Alison M. Rosen, "Moss Appeal: Mossimo Hits Target, Cheapskates Go Nuts!" *Orange County Weekly*, 2-8 March 2001.

Mossimo is now a Santa Monica-based design and licensing firm with 10 employees; it no longer manufactures, sources or directly markets its products. Target collaborates on design and is responsible for product development, sourcing, quality control, and inventory management. By adding a designer name to the product lineup, Target appears to be following the department store trend of competing with image, not just price. Robert Margolis, Chairman, President and CEO of Van Nuys-based Cherokee Inc. was personally involved in the Target-Mossimo deal. In March 2000 he stated in a press release, "A metamorphosis is taking place in American retailing whereby the leading retailers with skill sets like Target are doing their own sourcing, enabling them to provide much greater value to customers." Cherokee Inc. was also formerly an apparel and footwear manufacturer that now operates as a licensor and marketer of its brand.[45]

The shift in Mossimo's target markets–from high-cost boutiques and select department stores to a discount department store–is indeed a major one. Mossimo's year 2000 financial results were mixed, but generally showed an improvement over 1999. In April of 2001, Mossimo Giannulli, Chairman, President and CEO of Mossimo, Inc. stated, "We continue to be very pleased about our relationship with Target and remain excited and encouraged about our prospects for the future."[46] For the nine months ended September 30, 2001, Mossimo reported net income of $5.5 million under this new arrangement versus a loss of $12.6 million for the previous year.

The success of Target's and Giannulli's relationship is establishing a new business model that can reverse a pattern of failed licensing arrangements with designers. When Halston launched clothing and home furnishings lines in J.C. Penney stores in 1982, higher-end stores dropped his designer line, thus signaling the decline of his company. In July 2000, Sears announced the launch of an exclusive Benetton USA collection in 450 Sears stores; however, it was canceled before it opened due to Sears' disappointing apparel sales and Benetton's controversial advertisements.[47]

Nevertheless, developing brand loyalty remains the apparel manufacturer's greatest safeguard against the uncertain waters of consumer preferences, and one of these production relationships is the surest route to success available to a manufacturer today. To attain the consistent sales and reduced risks that branded manufacturers enjoy, manufacturers can: (1) develop their own brand which can be extremely costly; (2) contract with a brand name manufacturer; (3) produce for a private label retailer; or (4) become a licensee.

Some manufacturers fit roughly into one of the above classifications—brand-name manufacturer, private label manufacturer, licensee, or licensor. However, many more manufacturers work under a variety of classifications. For example, large firms, such as New York-based Liz Claiborne and Los Angeles-based Guess?, have established their own retail stores and outlets while continuing to sell their products to department stores. Outlets allow companies to sell excess stock and out-of-season or unpopular merchandise without taking the greater losses associated with selling through off-price channels. Los Angeles-based Lucky Jeans, 85 percent of which is now owned by Liz Claiborne, sells to department stores and off-price stores and

---

[45] "Cherokee Inc. Engineers Billion Dollar Licensing Agreement between Mossimo and Target," [press release on-line], 29 March 2000, available from *http://www.cherokeegroup.com*; Internet.
[46] "Mossimo, Inc. Reports Fourth Quarter and Fiscal Year 2000 Results."
[47] Valli Herman-Cohen, "Morphing from Mossimo to Mass-imo," *Los Angeles Times*, 4 January 2001.

simultaneously operates 33 stores of its own. Lucky Jeans is scheduled to open 21 more stores within the next year.[48] Manufacturers such as Nike, Tommy Hilfiger, and Calvin Klein, and retailers such as Macy's, all have merchandise designed and manufactured by Los Angeles-based firms.

Technology Changes

Los Angeles's apparel industry is made up of textile and apparel manufacturers, pattern makers, markers, graders, cutting services, equipment manufacturers, sewing contractors, package contractors, warehouses, distributors and others. Technology changes have permeated each of these industry segments, but the rate of widespread adoption has lagged behind other industries. Until the past decade, the technology of most apparel manufacturing processes was little changed from post-World War II apparel production.

However, a generally buoyant economy over the past several years created increased consumer demand for non-durable goods, especially apparel. With demand for apparel on the rise, the production cycle has drastically shortened over the past decade, and new products are now distributed to apparel retailers on a monthly basis. Some larger manufacturers can complete the production cycle in as little as 14 days, provided that the fabrics and trims are in-house. Technology has made this possible.

Indeed, larger manufacturers have been embracing new technologies over the last decade as computerization and automation have reduced labor costs and turnaround time. The "quick response" strategy previously mentioned encompasses such new technologies as computer-aided design (CAD), computer-aided manufacturing (CAM), Electronic Data Interchange (EDI), scanning, bar coding, labeling, and distribution. These enable manufacturers to provide "just-in-time production," which is now the *modus operandi* in apparel manufacturing.

However, most new technologies remain too costly for the small manufacturer. A single computer-aided design (CAD) workstation can cost as much as $35,000; grading, marking, plotting, cutting, and spreading machines cost more. Automating a factory floor can cost millions of dollars. About 90 percent of Los Angeles apparel manufacturers who work with major retailers use Electronic Data Interchange (EDI); however, only 30 percent of Los Angeles's designers use CAD, and even fewer manufacturers are engaged in computer-aided manufacturing (CAM).[49]

Business Management

Nearly all mid-to-large manufacturers have computerized their business-related departments, including purchasing (fabric and trim ordering), accounts receivable, accounts payable and payroll. Apparel industry-specific software tracks inventories and sales, monitors production, and analyzes costs for labor, materials and overhead. The volatile nature of the fashion industry today demands that firms adjust quickly to meet shifts in sales patterns as they occur, making

---

[48] "Brands Finding Payoff in Own Stores," *Women's Wear Daily*, 21 June 2001.
Metchek interview, 24 July 2001.

cost control critical to apparel firm operations. Forecasting tools help manage and improve efficiency. A firm's cost sheet usually reflects the entire production process (development, samples, patterns, fabric, trim costs, contract labor, cutting costs, indirect costs/overhead and hidden costs). [50]

As business management software packages become more affordable, smaller manufacturers are computerizing their business management systems, enabling them to operate more efficiently and cost effectively. Computer software packages for business management (including accounting, costing, inventory tracking, ticketing, various aspects of distribution and more) are more affordable than CAD and CAM systems. Today, production management software packages can be purchased for as little as four thousand dollars. Automation specialists such as Gerber Garment Technology Inc. have designed customer relationship management (CRM) programs that facilitate planning, scheduling and order-filling capabilities using just-in-time planning. They also allow users to manage their supply chain by tracking orders and inventory, thus improving margins and efficiency. Quick TruCost costing software, from Atlanta-based Methods Workshop, costs garments from the design stage onward to help determine profitability. Apparel Information Management System (AIMS), based in Santa Ana, California, offers software distribution and manufacturing systems for licensing fees ranging from $4,000 to $12,000, plus $1,000 for each additional user. AIMS also offers an EDI import/export integration engine starting at $4,000 plus monthly fees.

Production

Because the latest trends in production technology were outlined in a previous section on **The Apparel Production Process**, this section focuses mainly on technological changes that facilitate apparel production but are not directly related to it.

Large and mid-sized companies manage production through networked computers that join the design, fabric ordering, cutting, and production departments. Production management programs update modifications that occur during sample development. Each department updates the electronic specification (spec) sheet as they order the material and notions and complete each phase of the manufacturing process.

The Apparel Technology Research Center (ATRC) at California State Polytechnic University, Pomona has been engaged in the development of a zero inventory plant. This plant will feature a new zero inventory printing technology that significantly expedites the pattern making process. Zero inventory production grew out of the need to reduce inventories. The maintenance of inventories, especially those with short shelf life and little discount value, has become increasingly costly and risky for apparel manufacturers. Printed apparel has been especially risky because of the requirement for large print runs to decrease unit cost and the fickle nature of consumer tastes.

In response to this situation, the Beta Management Team (BMT) has developed a digital fabric printing system that requires no minimums and produces units fast enough to allow "on the fly replenishment" for hot selling items and minimum refill runs for slow movers. The benefits are

---

[50] Tate, *Inside Fashion Design.*

multiple: there is no printed fabric inventory; there is no "out-of-stock"; the cost benefits of volume cutting are retained; fabric designs are printed on demand; and the production of custom sizes are possible.

In addition, BMT's electro-static/digital printing technology prints several hundred times faster at one-half the cost than the ink jet printing equipment on the market today. BMT manager Bill Grier claims that it will revolutionize the local industry because it facilitates "production on demand," allowing for very short production runs and possibly making it uneconomical to source fabric outside the region in the future. Firms will obtain access to the technology through "deployment" of the equipment on an in-house rental basis. At 10,000 yards a month, the cost will be $6.50/yard.[51] However, some industry insiders are skeptical; potential users of the technology will need to make a costly investment in employee training, but no such training program is readily available as of yet.

The apparel industry has also begun to experiment with body scanning, but to date this technology has only been applicable to custom-tailored garments. With body scanning, three dimensional scanners map and measure a body in seconds; a computerized program then interprets the data points, displays an image and prints out the detailed measurements. Levi Strauss & Co. attempted to use it to mass produce custom-fitted jeans; however, this experiment received only a lukewarm customer response.

The Textile and Clothing Technology Corporation (TC²), a nonprofit research corporation based in Cary, North Carolina, has also developed body measurement technology. One of TC²'s goals is to shift the U.S. apparel industry from physical process supply chains to digital product supply chains. This new supply chain concept involves the digital integration of design and product development, marketing, manufacturing and sales, allowing the conversion of concept to product to take place much closer to the point of consumption than has been possible with traditional supply chains. Today, the dreams and the techniques exist for both of these potentially industry revolutionizing technologies; however, successful implementation has yet to happen.

Distribution

Electronic Data Interchange (EDI) has become the key technology for directly connecting retailers and manufacturers. Companies with EDI use a standardized computer network to electronically exchange routine business "transaction sets." Each different type of business document sent from a computer in one company to a computer in another company constitutes a transaction set; for example, purchase orders, invoices, status reports, and schedules would be different transaction sets. EDI features inventory "triggers" that will automatically place production orders, thereby optimizing a retailer's product assortment while avoiding over-stocks. Merchandise is delivered directly to the retailer's floor, rather than being stored in a warehouse at the retailer's expense.

---

[51] "New Manufacturing for the New Economy," BMT Business Plan, June 2001; phone interview with Bill Grier, President, Beta Management Team, 20 July 2001.

EDI has been standardized in the department store retail sector through adoption of the Voluntary Industry Communication Standard (VICS).[52] Although specialty boutique stores still do not use EDI, nearly all major retailers, including department stores and discounters, now use EDI. It is also widely used by the toy industry, grocers/supermarkets, insurance companies, education, entertainment, banking, and several federal government agencies.

While EDI is ideal for making production more efficient, it is also expensive. A complete system, which allows a business to interact with an unlimited number of clients and process an unlimited number of transaction sets, begins at $20,000 and can cost up to several hundred thousand dollars. In addition, users are assessed Value-added Network (VAN) charges based on the monthly document volume, and they must also pay a yearly maintenance fee of approximately $1,000. Other expenses include miscellaneous monthly and/or yearly fees, the cost of dedicated in-house staff, and technical support, which can cost anywhere from $100 to $250 an hour.[53]

An alternative to purchasing an in-house system is to outsource the EDI to a dedicated provider. Again, depending upon the number of transaction sets and the volume of inbound and outbound documents, it can cost as little as $1,500 (for a small manufacturer with three major clients/trading partners on the EDI system) to upwards of $10,000 monthly. Although $1,500 seems like a bargain, it adds up to $18,000 a year. For a manufacturer with less than $1 million in sales, EDI technology costs could run from two to seven percent of total revenues.[54]

For firms with fewer than three EDI partners, a web-based EDI is another option. Web-based EDI uses a high-speed Internet connection to deliver files to a client in a standard software format (i.e., a Microsoft Excel spreadsheet or a Microsoft Access database). A web-based EDI system requires no special software, dedicated staff, training, VAN charges, maintenance, or support contracts. For a company with three buyers and two transaction sets (e.g., invoices and purchase order numbers), this system would cost roughly $6,000 upfront and $250 per month for 100 document transmissions.[55]

New York-based QRS, formally known as Quick Response Services, provides PC-based and Web-based EDI packages, as well as mailbox and Internet EDI catalog services. QRS, a leading company in global sourcing and supply chain management, operates the largest Internet-based EDI catalog system for the apparel industry. Their website contains manufacturers' UPC (universal price code) numbers and enables retailers to place purchase order numbers directly. Small manufacturers not ready to bring EDI in-house can contract with QRS, which accepts paper invoices or regular e-mails from a manufacturer and translate the data into the EDI system for the retailers. It also translates the EDI data for the manufacturer into the format of their choice, and produces the appropriate barcodes and tickets. QRS's one-time set up fee is $300, plus a charge of $150 for each additional retailer.[56] However, each transaction accrues additional fees, and these can add up quickly.

---

[52] "Overview: The Department Store Industry."
[53] 1 EDI Source, Inc. based in Kent, Ohio, available from *http://www.1edisource.com*; QRS available from *http://www.qrs.com*.
[54] Anonymous interview.
[55] A needs/cost assessment was generated by 1 EDI Source, Inc. based on these specifics.
[56] Phone interview with EDI specialist Tomas Weeks at QRS Inc., 20 August 2001.

EDI systems primarily benefit retailers, not manufacturers. An in-house EDI system is the main option that benefits the manufacturer because it allows a retailer to transmit its selling reports every week to the manufacturer, enabling the manufacturer to track what has been sold by Stock Keeping Units (SKUs). SKUs delineate merchandise by style, color and size—details that add value to a production management system.

Inventory Management and Shipping

EDI systems can also connect the manufacturer with the warehouse. Unsold garments represent assets spent but not recovered; reducing stock held in warehouses is critical to profitability. EDI systems help to speed up the movement of inventory from the warehouse to the retailer. Computerized inventory systems allow the shipping department to know what is on hand in the warehouse, to pull orders for stores, and to ship garments according to a retailer's instructions.[57] Many smaller manufacturers, however, maintain their inventory in-house and ship directly to a buyer.

Supply Chain Management and Direct Distribution

The Internet and Web-based applications allow greater connectivity among firms and customers. E-mailing between manufacturers, designers and retailers is now a basic means of exchanging information, facilitating both communications and business transactions. Supply chain management software programs such as Fasturn's Operations Network (OPN) allow users to know the status and location of every item in the supply chain, be it fabric or trim, work in process, or finished garment.

Los Angeles-based Karen Kane described the impact of OPN as follows:

> OPN armed the production crew with full historical data that enabled increased efficiency in production planning and execution. Scheduling functionality kept everyone on track. End-to-end visibility encouraged collaboration between groups to meet end dates and reduce surprises for production. The twenty or so production [steps], 12 design steps, and dozens of data elements on average for each style were captured and documented. This advance communication allows production to be proactive. Additionally the captured knowledge was available at anytime even when key contributors are out of the office and helped eliminate miscommunication that can be problematic.[58]

Breakthroughs in "e-commerce" are not only opening new doors for retailers and apparel manufacturers to share more data on a business-to-business level, they are also providing new channels for designers, manufacturers, and retailers to market directly to consumers. Key retailing trends, including *multi-channel retailing, personalization,* and *value-added customer service,* are related to advancements in information technology.

---

[57] Tate, *Inside Fashion Design*.
[58] "Karen Kane Uses Fasturn's Operations Network Software to Improve Operations," 11 February 2002 [press release on-line]; available from *http://www.fasturn.com/wwwroot/press_release_09.shtml*; Internet; accessed 13 February 2002.

Multi-channel Retailing. The most competitive apparel manufacturers, marketers and retailers of the future will probably be selling through some combination of "bricks and clicks"—brick-and-mortar stores, catalogs and Web sites (both theirs and those run by others), as well as other media.

Catalog and Internet-based retailers have gained significant market share representing one out of every ten dollars spent on apparel in 2000. In 1999, on-line apparel retailers marked a major milestone when sales for the year topped $1 billion.[59] Out of the top 20 "e-retailers" in 2000, three were apparel firms. Known for its catalog, The Spiegel Group, which includes Eddie Bauer, was ranked number 16 with sales of approximately $175 million and 450,000 on-line customers. J.C. Penney filled the number 19 slot with over $150 million in sales and 5,000 customers. The number 20 spot went to The Gap (which includes Old Navy and Banana Republic) with more than $125 million in sales and 800 customers.[60]

Although Internet sales may seem impressive, web-based apparel retailing, not unlike mail order cataloguing, will probably never constitute the major percentage of total apparel retail sales. Most people do not want to purchase something that they cannot first try on. Potential customers are also concerned with the security of their credit card information, even though software programs have been created to safeguard against fraud.[61] According to Net Entrepreneur, between 30 and 60 percent of people who begin a purchase process on the Web actually complete the transaction over the phone, via fax, or by visiting a nearby store.[62]

From the retailer and manufacturer point of view, consumer purchases on the web are in such small quantities (usually one or two garments at a time) that processing orders can be unduly time-consuming. It is not cost effective to manage a website and process orders from a small number of individual buyers, especially for small manufacturers. From a designer's perspective, e-retailing has not proven as useful because wholesalers and retailers need to inspect clothing prior to purchase. Websites, however, have proven useful for showcasing designs and/or product lines and referring potential customers to locations where products are available.

There are, however, other options beyond maintaining individual websites. Companies such as Fashionmall.com and Styleclick.com, for example, offer ready-made selling forums, plus web content management support and order fulfillment services.[63] Both Fashionmall.com and Styleclick.com recently signed deals with Amazon.com and America Online, respectively, to offer apparel shopping via these on-line giants' sites. Apparel firms that contract with Fashionmall and Styleclick not only gain access to the potential customers visiting these virtual malls, but also to the millions more visiting Amazon and AOL.[64]

Personalization. The data that market researchers obtain about consumers and their buying habits are also being used to provide a higher level of tailored customer service. Customer

---

[59] "Retail Apparel Sales Statistics & Trends 1999-2000," About: Retail Trends [report on line]; available from *http://retailindustry.about.com/industry/retailindustry/ library/weekly/aa022200a.htm*; Internet; accessed 10 January 2002.
[60] "Top 100 Internet Retailers."
[61] Jules Abend, "21st Century Ushers in Greater Technology Optimization," *Bobbin Magazine*, January 2000.
[62] *Ibid.*
[63] Kathleen DesMarteau, "Retail IT: It's Not for Stores Anymore," *Bobbin Magazine*, September 1999.
[64] *Ibid.*

preferences are noted and customers are frequently invited to "special events" or alerted by mail or e-mail to items and/or sales of possible interest to them. "Cross-selling" of goods based on personal profiles is becoming increasingly the norm, and retailers and marketers both buy and sell profile databases.

Value-Added Customer Service. More retailers and manufacturers/marketers are realizing the value of providing "free" background information to consumers as part of their customer service programs. For instance, if a customer is in the market for skiwear, the best stores, virtual or otherwise, can be expected to provide slope information, weather and location tips. Consumers have come to expect this type of value-added service, based on their on-line shopping experiences.[65]

The past five years have seen major technological developments directly and indirectly connected to the apparel industry. Some of these technologies, such as the Internet, and advancements in CAD and CAM, are indeed transforming the industry and helping large manufacturers in particular to thrive. However, these new technologies, for the most part, remain inaccessible to the local industry's contractors. Hardware and software providers primarily target mid-to-large-sized manufacturers; affordable technology for smaller manufacturers/contractors is limited. Moreover, without appropriate training, investment in new technologies is not practical for the apparel workforce.

---

[65] *Ibid.*

FASHION FORWARD:
Assessing the Future of
Apparel Manufacturing in Los Angeles County

NAFTA and the Apparel Industry

The North American Free Trade Agreement (NAFTA) has definitely contributed to the movement of apparel production offshore. However, in considering the impact of NAFTA on the apparel industry in Los Angeles, some conceptual distinctions are necessary. First, while NAFTA seems to have exacerbated the movement of certain segments of apparel production to Mexico, it alone cannot be 'blamed' for this movement; that is, NAFTA has not set into motion massive capital flight from Los Angeles. The processes of reorganizing production and changing its associated geography began many years before NAFTA was realized.

Changes in the organization of production—the move to more 'flexible' production strategies—proliferated throughout the 1980's, causing vertical disintegration of the production process in certain apparel markets. In other words, it was no longer necessary for all stages of production to take place in the same location or even within the same firm. As communications and transportation technology improvements made offshore sourcing more feasible, firms that compete on a price basis have sought lower cost production locations. Technological changes facilitating offshore production were set into motion well before NAFTA. How the Los Angeles apparel industry has been affected by NAFTA must be considered in the context of this global reorganization and the changing geography of production. NAFTA cannot be blamed or praised as a sole causal factor, although there can be little doubt that it exacerbated this trend, especially among larger manufacturers.

Pre-NAFTA

Historically, apparel and textiles have been two of the most heavily protected U.S. industries. Ever since world trade in apparel and textiles began in the 1920's, textile companies have been highly successful at lobbying the government to support their interests; this influence remains. Tariffs and quotas have been the principal measures the U.S. has taken to protect local industry and restrict imports. Before multilateral trade policy in apparel emerged in 1974, U.S. trade negotiations were carried out bilaterally (i.e., country by country), ostensibly under the rubric of the General Agreement on Tariffs and Trade (GATT), the multilateral trading system established in 1947 in the wake of the Second World War. However, these bilateral negotiations were often in open defiance of GATT's principles.

The Multi-Fiber Agreement

The Multi-Fiber Agreement (MFA, also known as the "Arrangement Regarding International Trade in Textiles") governed trade in apparel from 1974 to 1994. It was conceived as an umbrella agreement under which importing and exporting nations could negotiate bilateral trade agreements. The stated goal in keeping with the GATT was to reduce barriers to trade. In actuality, each successive stage of the MFA imposed greater restrictions on trade as Western markets found the MFA inadequate for limiting the floods of low-cost Asian imports. Each time the MFA was renegotiated (in 1977, 1981, and 1986, followed by the Protocols of 1991, 1992, and 1993), restrictions were extended to more products, and new forms of protection were created. Exporting countries resisted these extensions of the MFA, but their lesser bargaining power in the negotiations thwarted their efforts to secure more advantageous trade policy.

In a "little Dutch boy and the dike" phenomenon, each attempt to stem the flow of imports into the U.S. simply sent foreign exporters probing for other weaknesses in the trade policy structure. The MFA simply tested their ingenuity. For example, the MFA stipulated that when a country's exports in a particular product category reached a certain share of U.S. imports in that category, then quotas and other restrictions would apply. Asian manufacturers found a number of ways to circumvent these trade restrictions. If Hong Kong's exports of cotton t-shirts to the U.S. reached a certain share of the U.S. market, then Hong Kong manufacturers might have done any of the following:

(1)   produced other kinds of cotton shirts;

(2)   made t-shirts of non-cotton material;

(3)   "trans-shipped" goods by sending them to a country whose quotas were not yet filled;[82] or

(4)   set up factories in other countries to sew cotton t-shirts for export to the U.S.

As early as the mid-1960's, trade policy had stimulated product diversification in Asia and encouraged shifts in the geography of apparel production; the MFA further propelled it. Hong Kong and others moved away from cotton products to synthetics and away from t-shirts to other types of clothing that were less strictly regulated.

Policy also promoted the development of apparel export industries in other countries in order to avoid quotas and tariffs and gain preferential access to the U.S. market. Because sewing shops do not require high start-up costs or long-term investment, the Asian Big Three of that era (Taiwan, Hong Kong, and the Republic of Korea) established sewing shops in many less developed countries in order to avoid quotas and tariffs on their domestic production. Thus, *the structure of trade policy encouraged the shifting of production to countries that had lower production costs*, adequate infrastructure, and a limited regulatory framework for apparel production and export.

The MFA eventually was replaced by the Agreement on Textiles and Clothing when the World Trade Organization (WTO) was created in 1995 during the Uruguay Round (URA) of GATT negotiations. In these negotiations, the U.S. agreed to reduce tariffs on apparel by an average of nine percent.[83] Consistent with the URA Agreement on Textiles and Clothing, all members of the WTO are in the process of phasing out all quotas over a 10-year period. On January 1, 2005,

---

[82] Trans-shipment of goods has been illegal since 1986.
[83] The U.S. Department of Commerce, Office of Textiles and Apparel is the source of the information quoted in *Industry and Trade Summary: Apparel*, U.S. International Trade Commission, Publication 2853, Washington D.C., January 1995.

the quota phase-out will be complete. When the quotas are phased out, apparel will be fully integrated into GATT and subject to the same rules as other sectors.

Caribbean Basin Economic Recovery Act

Trade policy also gave rise to the offshore sourcing of apparel. Since 1963, the U.S. tariff schedule has contained an item called "807" or "9802.00.80" that gives preferential duty treatment to goods *produced offshore of U.S.-made components*. This "production sharing" provision allows articles assembled offshore from U.S. components to enter the U.S. with duty taken only on the value added offshore. While acting as a stimulant to domestic supplier industries, it also encouraged U.S. and foreign firms to locate production (sewing) facilities offshore.[84]

Early on, larger apparel manufacturers in the U.S. took advantage of production sharing to gain a price advantage over competitors via low wage labor in less developed countries. What began as a trickle of investment in offshore sourcing in the 1960's became a flood in the 1980's and 1990's. Enabled by technological innovations in transportation and communications, firms shifted labor-intensive segments of production offshore in order to compete with cheaper foreign (largely Asian) imports and with other U.S. firms already using production sharing.

On August 5, 1983, President Ronald Reagan signed the Caribbean Basin Economic Recovery Act (CBERA) into law.[85] The CBERA (also called the Caribbean Basin Initiative or CBI) offered incentives for global manufacturers seeking low wage labor and access to the U.S. market to invest in the region. The CBERA guaranteed most goods produced in CBI countries preferential access to the U.S. market, but apparel was among a few excluded products.[86] In 1986 the U.S. implemented a "special access program" for CBI apparel goods. Called "807A," the special access program provided for reduced duties, but also guaranteed virtually unlimited quotas for apparel assembled in CBI countries.[87] Apparel entering the U.S. under "807A" must be made of U.S. fabric and cut in the U.S. before being sent to CBERA countries for sewing.

After Mexico signed the GATT in 1989, the 807A special access program was extended to it as well. Although Mexico had already been using the 807 provisions to export apparel produced domestically, Mexico's ability to take advantage of 807 production had been limited by quotas.

After Mexico gained parity with CBI in apparel, U.S. trade policy treated Mexico and CBI countries more or less as equals. Both had nearly unlimited quotas, and both had limited duties on 807 goods (only taken on value added). In order to access the U.S. market, both regions offered firms considerable and roughly equal incentives to engage in production sharing with the U.S.

---

[84] Technically written, for goods entering the U.S. under TSUS item 807/HTS 9802, duty is taken "upon the full value of the imported article, less the cost or value of such products of the United States." "Production Sharing," U.S. International Trade Commission, Publication 3 2243, December 1989, Appendix A4.

[85] " Production Sharing." The CBERA was enacted in title II of Public Law No. 98-67 and implemented by Presidential Proclamation 5133 of November 30, 1983, and applies to specified goods entering after January 1, 1984.

[86] *Caribbean Basin Economic Recover Act (14th Report 1998)*, U.S. International Trade Commission, Publication 3234, September 1999.

[87] *Ibid,* 13. The unlimited quota levels were called Guaranteed Access Levels, or GALs.

Although the CBERA and Mexico's parity stimulated production sharing arrangements, it simultaneously discouraged "full-package" apparel production in those or any other countries. Any apparel or textile goods entering the U.S. as non-807 products do not receive preferential treatment and are subject to MFA or other bilaterally negotiated restrictions. For example, a Hong Kong firm that sets up an 807 production shop in Mexico is required to purchase fabric from the U.S. rather than drawing upon its own textile market. This policy protects the U.S. textile industry.

The development of the apparel industry in CBI countries and Mexico supplemented the competitiveness of the U.S. industry by providing low wage labor inputs to an otherwise U.S. based industry. While the CBI discouraged competition between U.S. and CBI/Mexican apparel industry *suppliers*, it did place U.S. and CBI/Mexican apparel producers (or more accurately, U.S. and CBI/Mexican apparel production *workers*) in direct competition with each other.

The North American Free Trade Agreement

January 1, 1994, ushered in a new era in apparel trade policy in the Americas with the signing of the North American Free Trade Agreement (NAFTA). The main objective of NAFTA, as with other regional trade blocs, was to eliminate tariffs, quotas and other barriers among members. By 1999, the NAFTA countries—Canada, the United States, and Mexico—were well on their way to meeting this objective. Quotas no longer existed for qualifying goods, and tariffs had been reduced significantly.

The NAFTA agreement on apparel products has three basic elements: tariffs, quotas and rules of origin. The specific provisions of each, schedules for implementation, and products included are discussed below.

Rules of Origin

The NAFTA agreement on apparel and textiles is designed to create free trade in *originating* goods. Rules of origin, specifying which goods qualify for NAFTA benefits, are the crux of the apparel agreement.[88] Those goods not originating in NAFTA countries do not move 'freely' among NAFTA countries; goods that do not qualify for NAFTA treatment remain subject to each country's tariffs under the GATT/WTO or other bilateral agreements.

Rather than follow recommendations that NAFTA's rules of origin parallel those of the U.S.-Canada Free Trade Agreement, the negotiators of the NAFTA adopted some of the strictest rules employed in any free trade area.[89] The NAFTA stipulates that goods must pass a "triple

---

[88] With tariff rates already so low in 1993, NAFTA's main contribution to the shaping of apparel trade between the countries did not lie in tariff reduction. Moreover, as discussed below, most apparel goods entering Mexico before NAFTA entered under HS item 9802.00.80 for which there were no quotas.

[89] Gary Clyde Hufbauer and Jeffrey J. Schott, *North American Free Trade: Issues and Recommendations* (Washington, D.C.: Institute for International Economics, 1992), 277. Rules of origin are contained in Chapter 4 and appendix 401 of the NAFTA.

transformation test," or "yarn-forward test," in order to qualify for NAFTA treatment.[90] The yarn and all subsequent processing—weaving or knitting, cutting, and sewing—must be done in the U.S., Mexico, and/or Canada in order to qualify for NAFTA's reduced tariffs.

The effect of the yarn-forward test is greater protection for the North American textile industry, reflecting its continued significance as an industrial employer and its considerable political clout. Because neither foreign-made fabrics nor clothes made from such fabrics can receive NAFTA trade preferences, companies that want their goods to enter the U.S. market under NAFTA must use North American textiles.

Tariffs

Prior to NAFTA, U.S. tariffs on Mexico's main apparel exports to the U.S. were fairly low in comparison with average U.S. apparel tariff levels. U.S. tariffs on full-package apparel imports ranged from three percent for certain linen items on up to 34 percent, with garments of man-made fiber receiving one of the harshest tariff treatments—nearly 26 percent.[91] The overall average tariff on apparel imports was 19 percent; however, the weighted average pre-NAFTA tariff for Mexican apparel imports was only about six percent.[92]

The implementation of the NAFTA meant the automatic elimination of tariffs on about 30 percent of Mexican imports based on 1991 trade figures.[93] Production sharing goods no longer had duties when re-imported to the U.S.[94] Other apparel items traded between Mexico and the U.S. were divided into four basic staging categories[95] with tariff reductions scheduled to be phased in over a nine-year period. The category for a given commodity determined when its tariffs were to be lowered, and the staging categories corresponded to the sensitivity of the products with respect to U.S. industry.

Table 4-1 identifies the number and type of products falling within each staging category. By 1999, the majority of apparel commodities were traded freely. Currently, only the goods in Category C still have tariffs applied.

Though seeming small, the significance of the removal of tariffs should not be underestimated. The highly cost-competitive nature of the apparel industry means that tariffs, however low, remain an important cost consideration for high-volume manufacturers. Any cost-related advantage that a manufacturer can obtain over a competitor through its sourcing strategy can mean dramatic increases in sales for the former, and dwindling sales for the latter. Duties will remain for non-NAFTA countries, although several countries and regional blocs already enjoy

---

[90] *A Guide to the North American Free Trade Agreement: Implications for U.S. Business,* The U.S. Chamber of Commerce, International Division, 1992, 29. In contrast, the US-Canada FTA only used a "double transformation" test to determine originating goods, meaning that goods of foreign fabrics would have to be both cut and sewn in either country.

[91] *Industry & Trade Summary: Apparel.*

[92] Reuben Schwartz, "The Impact of the U.S.-Mexican Free Trade Agreement on Textile and Apparel Trade and Employment in the United States," in Peter Garber (ed.) *The Mexico-U.S. Free Trade Agreement* (Cambridge: MIT Press, 1994), 214.

[93] *Industry & Trade Summary: Apparel.*

[94] NAFTA, Appendix 2.4

[95] NAFTA, Appendix 2.1 Section B of Annex 300-B. All three NAFTA countries negotiated separate schedules with each other. This section focuses just on the U.S.–Mexico relationship, not the U.S.–Canada or the Mexico–Canada relationships.

duty-free (or almost free) relations with the United States (e.g., Israel) and with Mexico (e.g., Europe).

Table 4-1: NAFTA, United States Tariff Reduction Schedule[96]

Category	Duty Free	Commodities Affected	Selected Apparel Affected
A	1/1/94	185	Cotton underwear Foundation garments Pants & coats not of wool
B6	1/1/99	254	Men's & boys' knit coats of wool or cotton Most men's suits Babies' garments Hosiery
C	1/1/03	61	Men's coats and suit jackets of wool or FAH Women's sweaters, dresses, suits and blouses
D	Free	15	Ice hockey gloves Field hockey gloves

Quotas

Even though Mexico was not filling its quotas for most exports before NAFTA, NAFTA immediately eliminated quotas on 90 percent of U.S. apparel imports from Mexico that met NAFTA rules of origin. All remaining quotas are being phased out over a 10-year period. For those goods that do not pass the rules of origin test, quotas conform to MFA levels or to bilateral agreements. Exceptions have been made for some clothing assembled in Mexico of foreign fabrics that neither meets NAFTA rules of origin nor qualifies for NAFTA treatment. These products are assigned preferential tariff treatment up to particular levels, called tariff preference levels (TPLs). Normal, higher tariffs are then applied on quantities of imported product exceeding TPLs.

Quotas on apparel goods affect investment, production, and trade. Apparel is an industry in which the assembly stages are highly geographically mobile, an industry that competes more on the basis of cost than technological innovations. Policy changes creating manufacturing cost incentives can shift foreign direct investment away from more expensive production locations.

Given the quota elimination and tariff reductions associated with exporting to the U.S. from Mexico, one might have expected, with all other factors being equal, a rapid relocation of production to Mexico. However, U.S. content requirements (rules of origin) have mitigated the impact of tariff reductions, as has the cumbersome nature of navigating NAFTA provisions.

Nevertheless, the Los Angeles apparel industry has been impacted by NAFTA, although the extent of the impact has varied by industry segment. As will be discussed in greater depth in the

---

[96] This schedule applies to all originating apparel goods with the exception of tariff items contained in Schedule 2.1.B, which alters the tariff phase-out formulas for particular goods. An additional qualification limits the duty to 20 percent or below for any given year, which applies mainly to products with high tariffs for which the application of the above reduction formulas may result in tariffs exceeding 20 percent.

next section, high-end apparel manufacturers have witnessed only limited effects, whereas moderate-priced apparel manufacturers have restructured production in the past five years as a result of the advantages of production in Mexico. Even within the moderate market, some goods have been more likely to go offshore than others. Jeans production seems to have been moving offshore much more quickly than swimwear, for example. As noted above, each commodity seems to have its own particular dynamics, and NAFTA has affected each in different ways and to greater or lesser extent.

In brief, NAFTA has exacerbated a pre-existing phenomenon. It has facilitated the continuing movement of certain production operations from places like Los Angeles to Mexico by reducing the costs associated with manufacturing in Mexico. NAFTA has reduced the number of local production worker jobs, impacting some of the more vulnerable members of Los Angeles' working population—generally immigrants, predominantly female, with limited English and limited job skills—the working poor. Retraining these displaced workers is a policy challenge of the utmost importance. At the same time, some research has indicated that white-collar jobs in the apparel industry are actually replacing many of the lost production jobs, attenuating the overall employment decline

The next section explores the domestic effects of NAFTA on local apparel manufacturers.

FASHION FORWARD:
Assessing the Future of
Apparel Manufacturing in Los Angeles County

Survey of NAFTA's Impact on
the Los Angeles Apparel Industry

Since the passage of the North American Free Trade Agreement (NAFTA) in 1993, the Los Angeles apparel industry has seen a continuing erosion of its manufacturing base, especially in the production side known as "cut, make and trim." With the elimination of trade barriers and subsidies between the United States, Mexico and Canada, local manufacturers have increasingly outsourced their production to other countries. This practice has significantly hurt local contractors, shrinking their numbers and causing the loss of thousands of sewing machine operator jobs. Between 1995 and 1997 [the most recent year in which the California Employment Development Department (EDD) had disaggregated employment data], nearly 13,000 operator jobs disappeared. Based on this trend, the popular assumption had been that the apparel manufacturing base would all but disappear in Los Angeles. However, the same EDD employment data pointed to *a net increase in apparel-related white-collar employment* of nearly 18,000 jobs.

Anecdotal information suggested that certain segments of the local industry remained competitive despite the high cost of doing business in Southern California. These segments seemed to be made up of firms that occupy higher-end market niches; that is, manufacturers producing high quality fashion-forward goods in which price is not a deterrent for consumers. It also appeared that retailers' quick turnaround requirements and the increased use of technology were keeping a share of production close to home.

To determine the facts behind the anecdotes and to understand the EDD's conflicting job statistics, project staff undertook original research to more accurately assess NAFTA's impact on employment trends in the Los Angeles apparel industry. The availability of entry-level employment, along with the identification of occupations most in demand, those most difficult to fill, and reasons for any labor shortage, were examined. Also targeted for analysis was the extent to which NAFTA was creating new jobs. Findings appear in this section of the report and in **Employee Personnel Practices.**

Methodology

In the winter of 1999, a survey questionnaire was prepared and field-tested with human resource specialists and manufacturers in the local apparel industry. A database of randomly selected apparel manufacturers was developed based on information from Dun & Bradstreet. The goal was to obtain a stratified sampling of firms that would be representative of companies in the Los Angeles industry. Only companies with $5 million or more in annual revenues were selected, based on an assumption that smaller firms would not have the financial wherewithal or organizational capacity to establish offshore production facilities. Telephone interviews were conducted with Los Angeles area manufacturers between January and May of 2000. Interviews with a net total of 81 firms were secured. The breakdown of the final sample appears below.

Annual Revenues (in 000's)	# of Firms in Database	Sampling Goal	Actual # of Interviews
$5m- $9.9m	120	30 firms	24
$10m-$24m	125	33 firms	27
$25m-$49m	32	9 firms	16
$50m-$99m	17	5 firms	8
$100m or more	13	4 firms	6

A preliminary analysis of survey responses was completed over the summer of 2000. Follow-up on-site interviews were conducted with ten companies late in the year to determine whether any information had changed in the interim.

Firm Demographics

Based on the annual revenues of the 81 respondents, the average firm size was $36 million; however, the median size was actually closer to $18 million. Sixty-one of the firms, or 75 percent, manufactured women's apparel in the women's, missy or junior's category. Garments ranged from women's separates, dresses, and sportswear to coordinates and special occasion attire. Five firms specialized in swimwear; and a smattering of companies manufactured other specialty items like intimate wear and golf clothes.

Fifty-five of the companies, or 68 percent, manufactured apparel in the moderate-to-better category. Of these, thirteen companies produced exclusively in the "better" category of price points, and nineteen said they manufactured exclusively in the "moderate" category. In contrast, sixteen firms identified themselves as mainly or exclusively "budget."

Sixty-one of the respondents, or 75 percent, sold at least half of their apparel goods to department and specialty stores. Eight sold mainly to discounters, and another six sold mainly to budget stores. Four firms sold at least 30 percent of their goods through catalogs.

Major Findings

- *The size of a firm affects its ability to source offshore: the smaller the firm, the less likely it will shift production to Mexico or Asia.*

There were 24 companies in the revenue category of "$5 million to $9 million a year." Of these, thirteen manufacturers, or 54 percent, sourced solely in Southern California, while another ten companies, or 42 percent, had some offshore production. Interestingly, most of the offshore production went to Asia (seven firms), instead of Mexico (three companies). Many smaller companies acknowledged that they "cannot really monitor offshore production due to [the company's] size," indicating that size does affect ability to outsource production work.

The remaining 57 companies surveyed had $10 million or more in annual sales. The average was $49 million; the median was $25 million. Of these firms, 14 manufacturers, or 25 percent, kept all of their production in Southern California. The remaining 43 companies had some offshore production. Thirty-two firms, or 56 percent of the respondents, had production facilities in Mexico, while twenty-one companies, or 37 percent, outsourced their production in Asia.

- *Sourcing is increasingly global in scope.*

Manufacturers continued the trend of outsourcing production, mainly to Mexico and East Asian countries. Fifty-six percent of the respondents reported that they sourced some production in Mexico, compared to 48 percent in 1997 and 17 percent in 1992. It should be noted that in some instances production was being sourced in Mexico because a contractor with whom a manufacturer had a strategic relationship had relocated its operations south of the border. Thirty-seven percent of the companies surveyed sent some production to Asia, up from 27 percent in 1997 and 3 percent in 1992. Not surprisingly, as a result of this outsourcing, the number of contractors utilized per firm declined: 12 contractors per manufacturer in 2000, compared to 16 per manufacturer in 1997.

Of the 35 respondents who sourced in Mexico, 28 firms, or 80 percent, began sourcing right after NAFTA's inception in 1993. Twenty-eight manufacturers, or 69 percent, said NAFTA was a principal reason for their decision to move production to Mexico. However, when they were asked whether they planned to expand their operations in Mexico, only 14 firms, or 40 percent, said "yes." Another twelve firms said they would maintain their current level of production, while eight companies said they were not sure what they were going to do.

One manufacturer who had increased sourcing in Mexico over the past several years noted an escalation of that trend: "We used to cut everything in Southern California up until four to five months ago; now we send 90 percent to Mexico. We now cut in Mexico, deliver fabric and trims to Mexico…This has been an important development for us in the past twelve months."

Interviews with manufacturers indicated that few if any of them planned to decrease offshore sourcing and increase their Southern California production. Additionally, many manufacturers who had not sourced in Mexico avoided it because of perceived quality inadequacies. However, because production quality in Mexico has improved dramatically over the past decade, one more barrier—the quality barrier—to producing in Mexico is falling.

- *Manufacturers still maintain some production in Los Angeles.*

The extent to which production has moved offshore is the key to understanding NAFTA's impact. In this regard, the shift has not been as great as the public believes it to be. Twenty-nine companies, or one-third of the respondents, reported that they still had 100 percent of their production in Los Angeles. A total of 52 manufacturers, or 64 percent, kept at least two-thirds of their production in Southern California.

Of the firms that sourced offshore, only six reported that they had shifted *all* of their production outside of the United States. Another eight companies said that 75 percent or more of their production was done offshore. Based on these interview results, the majority of firms seemed to maintain a balanced sourcing policy by keeping some of their production in Los Angeles.

The following reasons were given for continuing to manufacture locally:

(1) Customer demand for quick turnaround of product and "small lot" production (i.e., limited production of specific items of clothing) made it impractical to produce offshore;

(2) "Face time" with contractors was needed in order to maintain quality control;

(3) A market niche in the higher price point categories made quality more important than price; and

(4) Small size and limited financial resources made it difficult to move production offshore.

Other manufacturers also indicated that sourcing in Southern California allowed greater control over production timing. One manufacturer explained, "Marking and grading require fast deliveries that we need. We need to do it here to be able to compete." That manufacturer used the example of a Mexico-based contractor that did not have a shipment ready. Because the manufacturer had local production facilities, they were able to re-cut and sew the order in-house, completing and shipping it within one week. This would not have been possible without a local plant.

- *Knowledge of NAFTA and offshore production has become a hiring criterion in some job categories.*

Nearly half of the firms currently sourcing in Mexico had advertised for and/or hired Southern California personnel who have NAFTA knowledge and expertise. More than 40 percent increased their personnel in jobs such as production management, quality control, import/export coordination, and data entry.

In contrast, only 16 firms reported lay-offs or decreased hiring as a result of NAFTA. Of these 16 manufacturers, half reported job reductions in blue-collar positions such as sewing, shipping and receiving, and warehousing.

Knowledge of NAFTA by import/export personnel enables a company to move its goods through customs in a timely fashion. One manufacturer articulated the frustration many manufacturers feel in working with customs agents: "Different agents require different documents; it's not standardized." Unless import/export personnel know how to navigate this complex system, merchandise can sit in customs at the U.S.-Mexico border for days or weeks, delaying shipments to retailers and causing manufacturers to lose sales.

- *Apparel firms have been slow to adopt new technology.*

Of the 81 respondents, 30 firms, or 37 percent, reported that they had websites. Survey respondents from another 11 companies said they did not know whether they had an Internet presence. Only 18 manufacturers, or 22 percent, reported that they had company e-mail accounts. Twelve companies said they were not sure whether they had e-mail, or if they did, the respondents did not know their own e-mail addresses.

Larger companies, especially those with considerable outsourcing experience, tended to use the Internet as an integral part of business operations. As one manufacturer stated, "We make extensive use of e-mail...because most of our customers have websites. We go on the Internet for shipping instructions....We are looking at a production development software (Gerber), possibly this year, which will allow specifications over the Internet. For example, a factory in Asia can log on and see the specifications....It will be much quicker and faster."

- *Computerization and technology have led to both job gains and losses.*

Computerization and technological advances in production methods have had mixed effects on employment numbers. Of the 55 firms that reported job gains or losses in specific categories, 11 respondents said that technology improvements led to staff reductions in front office/data entry and warehouse jobs. In contrast, 17 companies reported job gains in front office/data entry, e-commerce and information technology. Eight respondents cited job applicants' lack of technology skills as a major barrier to hiring. With the small number of respondents, however, these findings should be interpreted as suggestive, rather than indicative, of any major trends within the general population of manufacturers.

FASHION FORWARD:
Assessing the Future of
Apparel Manufacturing in Los Angeles County

Employer Personnel Practices

As economic integration continues, and NAFTA and other international treaties further impact trade, the Los Angeles apparel manufacturing industry will remain in a state of flux. Although the events of September 11[th97] appear to have temporarily slowed the offshore movement of "cut-make-trim" production work, this trend is expected to continue along with a steady decline in blue-collar jobs. The industry segments that will stay in Los Angeles are the ones that focus on trend-setting fashion, quick turnaround, and high quality.

While these "fashion forward" segments are continually being replenished with young designers coming out of the local design schools, many other jobs are going unfilled. As noted in an earlier section, there is a broad range of jobs in apparel manufacturing, and an even broader range associated with peripheral and supporting industries. Several of the manufacturers previously surveyed noted the "graying" of samplemakers and patternmakers, calling them "a dying breed." Others cited difficulties in hiring production managers ("most lack knowledge in offshore issues"), quality control staff ("most aren't familiar with the retailer's quality standards"), design assistants ("after working for one or two years they move on to another company"), and even sewing operators ("younger women aren't wanting to become sewers"). Still other jobs require an ever increasing level of technical skills as computerized design, manufacturing, and business software programs become an integral part of the industry.

In the interest of training and retraining industry workers for both current and future jobs, this section takes a closer look at industry wage expectations, career ladders, workforce demographics, and current recruiting and hiring practices.

Occupations and Wages

Occupations in the apparel manufacturing industry are usually categorized as either production or non-production, with each category having numerous sub-divisions. Based on 1997 data, 80 percent of the industry's workforce fell into 16 occupations, and more than 78 percent of all apparel industry employees were production workers.[98]

The largest single occupational title within the industry was garment sewing machine operators, accounting for 47 percent of total 1997 industry employment. Cutters, pressers (hand and machine), and pattern makers also made up a large segment of overall apparel employment. Additionally, non-production blue-collar occupations, such as packers, also included sizeable

---

[97] On September 11, 2001, Al Qaeda terrorists declared an unofficial "war" on the United States and American lifestyle by hijacking four "jumbo jet" airplanes and crashing two of them into New York's World Trade Towers and a third into the Pentagon in Washington, D.C. Over 5,000 people were killed.

[98] California Employment Development Department, Labor Market Information Division, 1997 Occupational Matrix [database on-line] available from *http://www.calmis.ca.gov*; Internet; accessed 20 December 2001.

numbers of workers. The largest white-collar occupations were clerks (traffic, shipping, and general office), general managers, top executives, supervisors, and sales representatives. *Table 6-1* summarizes employment numbers for the most significant occupations in 1997.

Table 6-1: Largest Apparel Occupations by Employment, Los Angeles County, 1997[99]

Occupational Title	1997	2004 (projected)	1997 Percent	1997 Cumulative Percent
Sewing machine operators - garment	52,780	46,770	47.2	47
Sewing machine operators – non-garment	5,123	5,054	4.6	52
Cutters and trimmers – hand	4,001	3,607	3.6	55
Traffic, shipping, receiving clerks	3,556	3,232	3.2	59
Textile operators, tenders	3,482	3,499	3.1	62
Hand packers and packagers	3,335	3,204	3.0	65
Pressing machine operators	3,135	2,587	2.8	67
Production inspectors, testers, graders	1,946	1,695	1.7	69
Pattern makers and layout workers	1,792	2,106	1.6	71
General managers, top executives	1,791	1,701	1.6	72
First-line supervisor/manager – production	1,554	1,509	1.4	74
Cutting, slicing machine operators, tenders	1,518	1,449	1.4	75
Sales representatives	1,441	1,379	1.3	76
Hand workers, not elsewhere classified	1,383	1,360	1.2	78
General office clerks	1,130	1,106	1.0	79
Pressers – hand	1,120	830	1.0	80
Total all occupations	111,891	102,857	100.00	100

Source: California Employment Development Department, LMID, 1997 Occupational Matrix

Most employees work on a full-time basis. Interviews with manufacturers or contractors suggested that companies might prefer to lay off workers before resorting to part-time work. When the seasonal production is extremely busy, workers may work overtime.

Wages tended to be correlated with perceived occupational skill level, with production workers generally earning less than non-production workers. After management, designers were paid the highest wages, sewers the lowest, and falling in between were patternmakers, pressers, spreaders, and cutters. Overall, people working in the apparel industry made on average $22,670 in 1999 nationwide. The median hourly wage was $8.22 and the mean was $10.90.[100]

Most occupational titles reflect the stage of production associated with the job. Hence, the definition of production stages in a previous section of this report explains the occupations. Wage data included in this section came from two main sources: Occupational Employment Statistics 1999 National Industry-Specific Wage Estimates[101], and the Los Angeles Apparel

---

[99] This table provides only a partial listing of occupations since the LMID does not track all jobs by industry. For example, fashion designers are tracked separately in the broader occupational category "Designers, Except Interior Designers," which also includes graphic designers, product designers, set designers, etc.

[100] "1999 National Industry-Specific Occupational Employment and Wage Estimates," U.S. Department of Labor, Bureau of Labor Statistics, Occupational Employment Statistics [database on-line]; available from *http://www.bls.gov/oes/1999/oessrci.htm*; Internet; accessed 28 February 2001.

[101] *Ibid.*

Industry Wage and Occupational Survey 1998 Report.[102] The first estimated industry wages on a national scale, and the second did the same for the Los Angeles region, drawing upon an independent survey of manufacturers and contractors. While more current numbers are not yet available, in September 2001 the Los Angeles County Economic Development Corporation reported only 38,000 jobs in the "cut and sew" category, with just 10 percent of these being low-paying entry level positions.[103]

Management and Administrative Staff: Most management and more highly skilled administrative staff are paid as salaried employees. The average annual salary of management employees was $69,570.[104] Excluding Chief Executive Officers (CEOs), their hourly wages ranged between $24.00 and $37.00. It was estimated that CEOs earned in excess of $53.00 per hour, or $100,870 annually.[105] Business and financial operations employees made on average $22.74 hourly, ranging from just under $18.00 for training specialists to nearly $32.00 for financial specialists.[106] Administrative support occupations averaged about $11.50 per hour, ranging from about $9.00 for file clerks to almost $18.00 for administrative supervisors.[107]

Designers: A designer's compensation can be unlimited based on the sales performance of the products s/he designs. If the products bring significant sales to the company, then overall compensation can increase with bonuses. Designers accounted for less than one percent of overall employment in apparel manufacturing and averaged about $50,800 in annual earnings (about $24.42 hourly).[108]

The production occupations listed below accounted for more than 68 percent of apparel employment.

Patternmakers: Patternmakers generally earned between $10.00 and $25.00 per hour depending upon their level of experience and the size of the company.[109] Their average hourly wage was $14.36, amounting to about $29,860 annually.[110] Both "first patternmakers" and "production patternmakers" fell into two general categories: those who made patterns by hand and those who used CAD programs. The latter category tended to pay better than the former.

Graders: Graders earned between $12.00 and $20.00 per hour.[111] Wages depended upon company size, individual experience, and CAD proficiency.

---

[102] Linda J. Wong, "The Los Angeles Apparel Industry Wage and Occupational Survey 1998 Report" (Los Angeles: Community Development Technologies Center, 1998) reports findings from an extensive survey of manufacturers and contractors in the apparel industry.
[103] "Manufacturing in the Los Angeles Five-County Area."
[104] "1999 National Industry-Specific Occupational Employment and Wage Estimates."
[105] *Ibid.*
[106] *Ibid.*
[107] *Ibid.*
[108] *Ibid.*
[109] Wong, "The Los Angeles Apparel Industry Wage and Occupational Survey, 1998 Report."
[110] "1999 National Industry-Specific Occupational Employment and Wage Estimates."
[111] Wong, "The Los Angeles Apparel Industry Wage and Occupational Survey, 1998 Report."

Markers: Wages for markers also tended to correlate with computer capabilities. They earned between $10.00 and $22.00 per hour[112] depending upon company size, individual experience, and CAD proficiency.

Cutters: Cutters earned between $6.50 and $15.00 per hour, with cutting managers earning slightly more.[113] Cutters' average hourly wage was $9.07, or about $18,860 annually.[114] Wages varied based upon company size and individual experience. Hand and computerized cutters did not appear to earn significantly different wages.

Sewers: Accounting for about 42 percent of all apparel industry employment, sewers earned between $7.10 and $9.21 per hour nationally, with girls' outerwear and miscellaneous fabricated textile products respectively at the lower and higher ends of the range.[115] The national average wage for all sewers was $7.74 per hour or $16,090 annually.[116] Hand sewers earned slightly more, and custom sewers (tailors) earned about $19,360 on average.[117] Los Angeles firms paid an estimated $5.75 to $9.00 per hour for sewing machine operators, and between $6.00 and $10.00 for overlock machine operators.[118]

Workers must be paid at least the minimum hourly wage to comply with state and federal labor laws. However, rather than paying workers a flat hourly rate, many manufacturers and contractors prefer to use the piece-rate system, which creates incentives for worker speediness and productivity. Sewers who work at "piece-rates" are paid according to the number of finished pieces that meet quality standards, rather than their actual hours worked. In this remuneration system, any errors and defects (and any time spent on these) do not count toward earnings. Some work may also be disallowed if a piece has a fabric flaw.

Quality Control: Quality control workers accounted for about three percent of the apparel workforce and earned on average $9.29 per hour or $19,310 annually.[119] Los Angeles firms paid quality control workers between $6.00 and $16.00 per hour depending upon company size, individual experience, and CAD proficiency.[120]

Other production occupations, such as spreaders, pressers, sample makers and finishers all earned roughly the same as sewing machine operators.

Remuneration systems among apparel firms differed considerably. Many contractors and manufacturers indicated that production workers were paid at piece-rate wages, whereas other

---

[112] *Ibid.*

[113] *Ibid.*

[114] "1999 National Industry-Specific Occupational Employment and Wage Estimates."

[115] "Career Guide to Industries," U.S. Department of Labor, Bureau of Labor Statistics [report on-line]; available from *http://www.bls.gov/oco/cg/home.htm*; Internet; accessed 20 December 2001.

[116] "1999 National Industry-Specific Occupational Employment and Wage Estimates."

[117] *Ibid.*

[118] Wong, "The Los Angeles Apparel Industry Wage and Occupational Survey, 1998 Report"; and "Los Angeles-Long Beach MSA Occupational Employment and Wage Data, 1999," California Employment Development Department, Labor Market Information Division [database on-line]; available from *http://www.calmis.ca.gov*; Internet; accessed 20 December 2001.

[119] "1999 National Industry-Specific Occupational Employment and Wage Estimates."

[120] Wong, "The Los Angeles Apparel Industry Wage and Occupational Survey, 1998 Report."

manufacturers, especially in the higher-end market, paid employees hourly wages. Union shops paid hourly wages according to the negotiated union contract.

Consumer Concerns

Although all wages listed above indicate payment at or above the prevailing minimum wage at the time the surveys were conducted, a two-tiered industry does exist. Legitimate manufacturers and contractors follow Fair Labor Standards regulations. However, others, who operate in the "underground economy" may resort to abusive labor practices in order to produce garments at lower prices.[121] The 2000 survey published by the U.S. Department of Labor's Wage and Hour Division showed only limited compliance with wage and hour laws among the Southern California firms it monitored or inspected. *Table 6-2* summarizes the results.

Table 6-2: Compliance with Wage & Hour Law in Los Angeles Apparel Firms

Compliance Category	Percent of Firms in Compliance			
	1994	1996	1998	2000
Both Minimum Wage and Overtime	22	39	39	33
Overtime	22	45	46	40
Minimum Wage	39	57	52	46
Child Labor Laws	96	100	100	97
Homework prohibitions	83	93	96	94
Record Keeping provisions	26	36	49	44

Source: U.S. Department of Labor, Wage and Hour Division, "Apparel Industry, Southern California, Survey 2000," presented in August 2000.

Child labor and homework were the only categories in which firms approached full compliance. Only 46 percent of all firms inspected followed minimum wage laws, and 40 percent followed overtime requirements.

Apparel production is highly seasonal, with a new fashion "season" emerging every two months. The seasonality of demand means that during certain seasons, workers are required to work extremely long hours to fill orders; during other times of the year, they may work part-time, if at all. For example, summer active-wear has its big production season from January to June, after which production workers are laid off until the next season. Coats are manufactured from July to January, with lay-offs occurring thereafter. In order to accommodate these seasons, seasonally specialized firms (such as swimwear or coats) establish flexible employment situations, such that employment may increase significantly during certain seasons and decline steeply during others.

The budget market is especially prone to wage and hour violations since it is structured in such a way that "sweatshop" conditions are virtually inevitable. Domestic firms producing for this labor-intensive end of the apparel industry must compete against Mexican factories. Many have relied on a poorly paid workforce as a means of remaining competitive.

---

[121] Tate, *Inside Fashion.*

Both state and federal regulations have attempted to correct this situation. In 1999, Governor Gray Davis signed into law Assembly Bill 633, which was the first legislative attempt to hold manufacturers responsible for the unpaid wages of contractors' employees. Supporters heralded its passage as "a huge breakthrough for thousands of garment workers," and "the toughest garment manufacturer's responsibility law in the country."[122] Manufacturers associations, while perhaps not enthusiastic about the legislation, worked with labor advocates and retailers to pass the bill.

Since its passage, however, many worker advocates have criticized it as too weak. While AB 633 does make manufacturers responsible for contactors' failure to pay wages to their employees, these employees are not given the right to sue manufacturers or retailers to recover their wages. Indeed, since its passage, the state has recovered only a small amount of money from manufacturers in unpaid wages, and labor law violations in Los Angeles have actually increased.[123] In addition, disagreement exists about whether retailers are indeed liable: the California Retailers Association asserts that the law does not apply to retailers, that it covers only companies that "buy fabric."[124] The issue of liability for wages and working conditions between manufacturers and their contractors has not yet been resolved, and the problem continues.

Federal regulations pertaining to overtime pay have changed some of these practices, however. Current regulations mandate that a worker earn overtime pay for any hours worked beyond eight per day regardless of the total hours for the week. During the first quarter of FY 2000, the U.S. Department of Labor recovered over $400,000 in back wages for 867 garment workers. [125] These regulations have hit contractors especially hard because they operate on inconsistent volumes, often processing large orders quickly and without advance notice. Regulations have also contributed to the movement of production jobs offshore where wages are lower and working conditions less closely monitored.

However, the consumer activism that began spotlighting apparel industry abuses in the 1990's has made it more difficult for retailers, licensors, and manufacturers to knowingly source from non-compliant contractors and suppliers, wherever they are located. These global efforts have called for accountability at every stage of the production process, demanding that workers receive livable wages and be provided safe and humane working conditions.[126]

Major retailers and designers such as Nike have been forced to respond, and in many cases are working to ensure that their factories, and those of their contractors, are not violating labor laws. In 1998 the American Apparel Manufacturers Association[127] founded the Worldwide Responsible Apparel Production (WRAP) program, which is establishing a certification and

---

[122] "California Adopts Toughest Sweatshop Law of its Kind in the Country," *Sweatshop Watch* [newsletter on-line] 29 September 1999, available from ***http://www.sweatshopwatch.org***; Internet.

[123] Nancy Cleeland and Marla Dickerson, "Davis Cuts Requested Labor Law Funding," *Los Angeles Times*, 27 July 2001; and Aurelio Rojas, "Sweatshops Still in Business: Reform Law Fails to Slow Abuse by Garment Makers," *Sacramento Bee*, 28 January 2001. According to the U.S. Department of Labor, only 33 percent of the companies inspected in the garment industry in 2000 were in compliance with federal minimum wage and overtime laws compared to 39 percent in 1998.

[124] Rojas, "Sweatshops Still in Business."

[125] "No Sweat," U.S. Department of Labor Garment Enforcement Report, October 1999–December 1999 [report on-line]; available from ***http://www.dol.gov/dol/esa/public/nosweat/garment17.htm***; Internet.

[126] Activist groups include Sweatshop Watch in Oakland California and The Garment Worker Center in Los Angeles.

[127] Now American Apparel & Footwear Association.

compliance program that will independently monitor apparel manufacturers and certify them if their facilities meet the WRAP Principles.

However, because the majority of production is outsourced, it is difficult to monitor, let alone detect, violations. Although the U.S. Department of Labor still employs its compliance monitoring force, its sweatshop monitoring program called "No Sweat" has been dropped. And, while the movement to eliminate all labor and safety violations in the apparel industry continues, the latest report from the Department of Labor indicates only "limited impact."[128]

Demographic Characteristics

Industry demographics shed some light on why segments of the workforce have been vulnerable to the violations cited above. Bonacich and Appelbaum estimated that approximately two-thirds of the apparel workforce was female. Men tended to be cutters and pressers and women tended to be trimmers. They noted that recent data indicated that nearly 50 percent of sewing machine operators were male, which is especially interesting since sewing was previously female-dominated.[129]

Historically, the apparel industry has provided employment for each new wave of immigrants, and this trend continues today. Research conducted in 1998 indicated that at least two-thirds of Los Angeles apparel employees were Latino, making Latinos the largest ethnic group.[130] Even though Latinos made up the largest ethnic group in most companies, some evidence linked ethnic composition of the workforce to company size. Among manufacturers with under $1 million in revenue, non-Hispanic whites were the second largest group (16 percent), followed by "other" (8 percent), and Asians (7 percent). For manufacturers earning between $1 million and $10 million, the second largest ethnic group was Asians (25 percent) followed by non-Hispanic whites (6 percent), and "other" (2 percent). Firms above $10 million showed non-Hispanic whites as the second largest ethnic category, followed by Asians, and "other."

Overall, more than 66 percent of apparel workers in 1990 were Latino, with the largest group being Mexican. More than 14 percent of industry employees were Asian, and slightly more than eight percent were of European ancestry. However, people of European ancestry dominated the white-collar occupations, accounting for nearly half of all white-collar workers. In contrast, 75 percent of operatives and 73 percent of laborers were Latino. Asians, while more concentrated in white-collar occupations, were also represented in blue-collar occupations: 31 percent of white-collar workers and about 13 percent of blue-collar workers in the garment industry were Asian.[131]

---

[128] Mary McKnight, Western Region Garment Coordinator, U.S. Department of Labor, ESA Wage & Hour Division; phone interview conducted 14 February 2002. Per McKnight, those firms that are monitored comply; however, the compliance monitoring force is not large enough to inspect all local apparel firms.

[129] Bonacich and Appelbaum.

[130] Wong, "The Los Angeles Apparel Industry Wage and Occupational Survey, 1998 Report."

[131] Bonacich and Appelbaum, 169. Data taken from the *Bureau of the Census, Public Use Microdata Sample for Los Angeles, 1990* was analyzed by the authors. Current statistics are not yet available.

Although ethnicity does not necessarily have implications for job hiring, training, or advancement, language skills do affect the process. Many garment workers are drawn from recent immigrant populations that have limited English skills. For many workers with limited English skills, apparel is one of the few industries that offer job opportunities.

Career Paths

Information about career paths and advancement opportunities within the apparel industry tends to be limited. Even some of the largest apparel firms lack formal career ladders. Diverse titles for jobs with similar responsibilities also muddy the picture.

The California Department of Education's Department of Home Economics Careers and Technology publishes the following list of careers in fashion design, manufacturing, and merchandising:

Entry level jobs (after high school graduation): Fashion Design Aide, Fabrics/Accessories Estimator, Sales Associate, Fashion Advisor, Visual Displayer, Costumer Assistant

Technical jobs (requires post-secondary education): Assistant Designer, Fashion Illustrator, Textile Technician, Computer Imaging Consultant, Merchandise Displayer, Fashion Buyer

Professional jobs (requires college/university/postgraduate education): Fashion Designer, Fashion Journalist, Cloth Designer, Wardrobe Supervisor, Fashion Artist, Fashion Merchandising Manager

Certain career ladders can be inferred from these listings; for example:

Wholesale:	Fashion Design Aide → Assistant Designer → Fashion Designer → Owner
Retail:	Sales Associate → Fashion Buyer → Merchandise Manager → Store Manager

The list presents a very limited picture, however: many of these positions relate to the retail sector, and apparel production jobs other than design appear nowhere on the list. Nevertheless, the list does underscore the role additional education and training play in career advancement.

The January 25, 2002 issue of *California Apparel News* ran 113 "help wanted" ads for 135 jobs.[132] Eighteen listed sales positions; 16 advertised positions for designers, assistant designers, or textile designers; 15 sought patternmakers or pattern technicians; and 12 were looking for production managers or assistant production managers. Of the 135 jobs, only five indicated they would consider entry-level applicants, and three of those expected a candidate to possess relevant industry knowledge. Previous experience was a consistent criterion. Moreover, the majority of

---

[132] "Positions Available," *California Apparel News* [newspaper on-line], 25 January 2002, available from *http://www.apparelnews.net/Class/Ads/009positions.html*; Internet; accessed 29 January 2002.

the ads specified computer skills, and many employers sought applicants with knowledge of industry-specific software.

Again, certain career ladders could be teased from the required skill sets in these ads. For example, criteria for jobs in accounting/finance indicated the following potential paths:

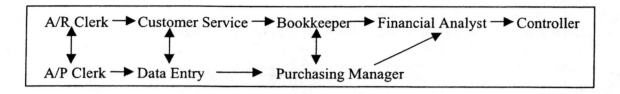

Production supervisory and management job descriptions painted the following picture:

Production Coordinator → Asst. Production Manager → Production Manager

Although a few production manager slots required knowledge of the domestic market only, the majority expected applicants to be experienced in both domestic and offshore production (primarily Mexico) and to be bilingual in Spanish and English. It also appeared as if opportunities existed for a production manager to become an operations manager, and possibly even general manager or owner.

However, moving up a career ladder reflects not only what an individual knows but also whom that individual knows. In the 1998 survey of manufacturers and contractors, approximately two-thirds of apparel companies affirmed that advancement opportunities existed within their organization. However, they also acknowledged that internal opportunities to move up a career ladder were fairly limited, due, in part, to the small size of most firms. Firms usually only promoted someone when a higher position was vacated, which might not occur very frequently.[133] Limited advancement opportunities provide an incentive for ambitious individuals to begin their own firms. As noted in a previous section, many firms share overlapping histories as designers, sales agents, and others with entrepreneurial spirit have left existing companies to become independent manufacturers or contractors.

For example, someone beginning as a sewing machine operator might pursue one of the following career paths. (*See Figure 6.1.*) Following Path A, a sewing machine operator is trained to use an overlock machine. As an overlock operator, s/he may move up to the position of supervisor, and/or receive training to become a sample maker. After mastering sample-making, s/he may learn the basics of pattern making (first pattern maker), and eventually move on to become a production pattern maker, a computer pattern maker (with additional CAD training), a design room coordinator, or a computer grader (also with CAD training). After mastering pattern making and grading, the former machine operator can open his/her own pattern making and grading business.

---

[133] Wong, "The Los Angeles Apparel Industry Wage and Occupational Survey, 1998 Report."

Figure 6.1:

APPAREL INDUSTRY CAREER PATHS IN CONTRACTING FROM PRODUCTION TO ENTREPRENEUR

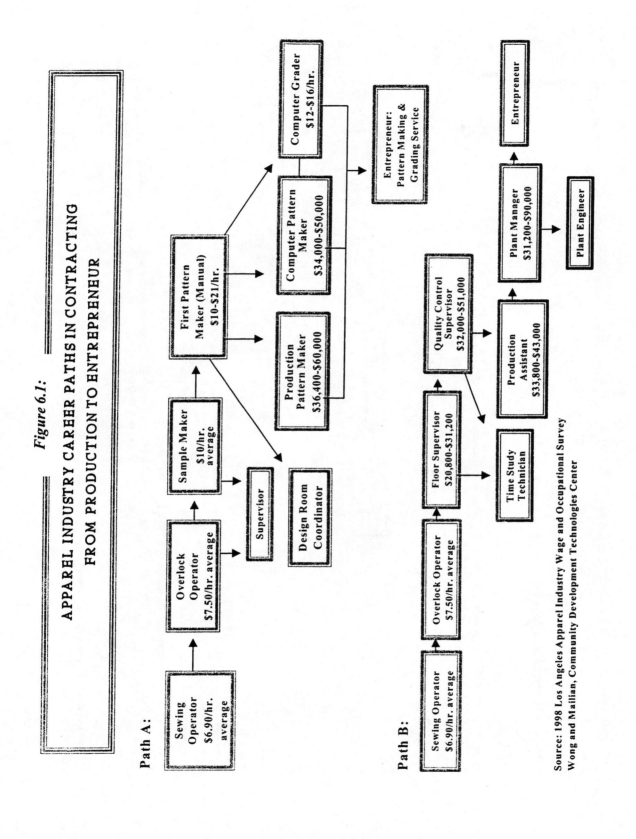

Path A:

Sewing Operator $6.90/hr. average → Overlock Operator $7.50/hr. average → Sample Maker $10/hr. average → First Pattern Maker (Manual) $10-$21/hr.

Overlock Operator → Supervisor

Sample Maker → Design Room Coordinator

First Pattern Maker → Computer Grader $12-$16/hr.

First Pattern Maker → Computer Pattern Maker $34,000-$50,000

First Pattern Maker → Production Pattern Maker $36,400-$60,000

Computer Pattern Maker / Production Pattern Maker → Entrepreneur: Pattern Making & Grading Service

Path B:

Sewing Operator $6.90/hr. average → Overlock Operator $7.50/hr. average → Floor Supervisor $20,800-$31,200 → Quality Control Supervisor $32,000-$51,000

Floor Supervisor → Time Study Technician

Quality Control Supervisor → Production Assistant $33,800-$43,000 → Plant Manager $31,200-$90,000 → Entrepreneur

Plant Manager → Plant Engineer

Source: 1998 Los Angeles Apparel Industry Wage and Occupational Survey
Wong and Mailian, Community Development Technologies Center

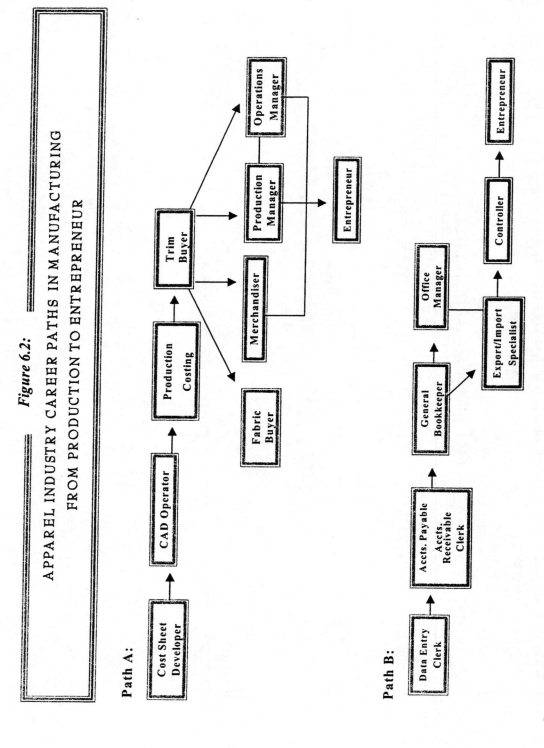

Figure 6.2:

APPAREL INDUSTRY CAREER PATHS IN MANUFACTURING
FROM PRODUCTION TO ENTREPRENEUR

Path A:

Cost Sheet Developer → CAD Operator → Production Costing → Trim Buyer

Trim Buyer → Operations Manager

Trim Buyer → Merchandiser

Trim Buyer → Production Manager

Trim Buyer → Fabric Buyer

Production Manager → Entrepreneur

Path B:

Data Entry Clerk → Accts. Payable Accts. Receivable Clerk → General Bookkeeper → Office Manager

General Bookkeeper → Export/Import Specialist → Controller → Entrepreneur

Source: 1998 Los Angeles Apparel Industry Wage and Occupational Survey
Wong and Mailian, Community Development Technologies Center

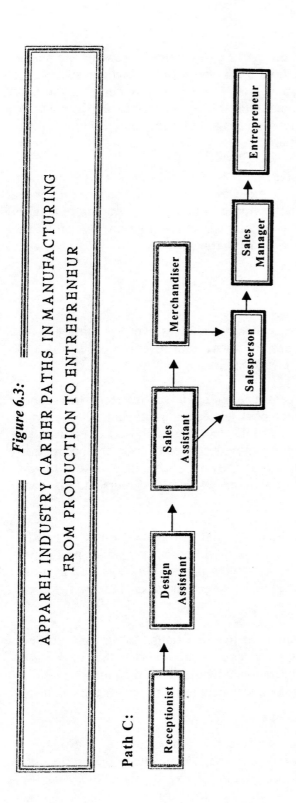

Figure 6.3:

APPAREL INDUSTRY CAREER PATHS IN MANUFACTURING
FROM PRODUCTION TO ENTREPRENEUR

Path C:

Receptionist → Design Assistant → Sales Assistant → Merchandiser

Sales Assistant → Salesperson → Sales Manager → Entrepreneur

Merchandiser → Salesperson

Source: 1998 Los Angeles Apparel Industry Wage and Occupational Survey
Wong and Mailian, Community Development Technologies Center

Path B provides a different scenario. According to this path, a single needle sewing operator is trained as an overlock operator and then may become a floor supervisor. As floor supervisor, s/he may move into the position of quality control supervisor. From quality control, s/he may become a production assistant or a time study technician. Production assistants may move up to plant management. With further training and experience, the plant manager may become a plant engineer, or may decide to manage his/her own company.

While career ladders do exist in the apparel industry, moving from blue- to white-collar occupations is difficult because moving up each rung requires added training and experience. Moreover, moving up to any computer-related job (for example, computerized grading or pattern making) requires considerable formal training. The training programs that are available are discussed in **Findings from the Education and Training Inventory.**

Employer Hiring Practices[134]

Because most apparel firms are fairly small, business owners themselves overwhelmingly make hiring decisions. However, in larger companies (especially those with revenues exceeding $10 million) hiring and recruitment may be delegated to department managers.

Apparel manufacturers generally recruit new employees through employee referrals, newspaper advertisements, or employment agencies. They either post job openings in trade publications and ethnic newspapers or use the California Employment Development Department and other agencies for recruitment purposes. The hiring strategy generally depends upon the occupation for which they are hiring: for white-collar occupations, they may advertise in *California Apparel News* or other trade publications, whereas they may use ethnic newspapers and informal networks to fill blue-collar jobs.

In contrast, contractors primarily use informal networks, especially word-of-mouth, to recruit new employees. Relatives of existing employees are often favored. Some companies post signs on their buildings announcing openings or run ads in ethnic newspapers. Owners hire in most companies, but in larger companies hiring is delegated to department or human resource managers.

Most manufacturers require experience above all else in their job applicants. In the 2000 survey of NAFTA's impact on local apparel manufacturers, most companies reported that they were reluctant or unwilling to hire entry-level employees for non-sewing machine operator jobs. Slots in shipping and receiving were the only other occupational categories for which the majority recruited at the entry-level.

Nearly all firms required experienced personnel in white-collar job categories. However educated they might be in techniques for their particular job, applicants who are recent graduates—even graduates of the Fashion Institute of Design and Merchandising or Los Angeles Trade Technical College—lack experience working in the industry. Tellingly, many

---

[134] Taken from Wong, "The Los Angeles Apparel Industry Wage and Occupational Survey, 1998 Report."; and the 2000 survey of NAFTA's impact on Los Angeles apparel manufacturers.

manufacturers hired not from design schools and manufacturing training programs, but from word-of-mouth referrals and by luring employees from other manufacturers.

Employers also underscored the importance of English language proficiency, adequate formal education, and computer skills as minimum requirements for all jobs. Unfortunately, the majority of production employees in the apparel industry are first generation immigrants. As such, they lack basic English communication skills and may even be non-literate in their native language.

One manufacturer highlighted the overall lack of basic skills among many job applicants, even those who were college graduates applying for white collar positions. This manufacturer administers a test for all entry-level applicants in which they are asked to write a paragraph, perform simple addition and multiplication, and answer basic apparel-related questions. Many applicants do miserably, exhibiting lack of proper English grammar, an inability to construct a complete sentence, and poor math skills. When asked to multiply 6 by 12, one applicant had categorized this basic calculation as "higher math." The manufacturer commented that the overall skill level among entry-level applicants in the industry is "disturbing and pathetic."

Almost half of the firms surveyed underscored the lack of "qualified," "skilled," "experienced," or "trained" applicants for jobs in design, patternmaking, engineering, production management, quality control, and sales. Additionally, several manufacturers who produce swimwear, evening dresses, and other specialized merchandise noted that few, if any, training programs provide training specific to their industry niche. Because fabrics used in swimwear and evening dresses require special handling, they often have difficulty hiring people with the skills needed to work in these specialized areas.

Companies that provided in-house training did so through their mid-level management employees or seasoned veterans. Most of the training was informal, in some cases, even haphazard. None provided vocationally specific English language training or basic skills training; few provided any formal skills upgrading. Most relied on the educational system to provide employees with needed skills.

Year	Federated Department Stores	May Company	Saks Inc.	Dillards (private company)
1988	Campeau Corp. acquired Federated. Foley's and Filene's sold. Goldsmith merged into Rich's. Macy's purchased Bullock's and I.Magnin from Campeau.	Acquired Foley's in Houston and Filene's in Boston	Acquired 5 Lovemans stores (TN)	
1989		Merged with O'Neil's. Seven Goldwaters' stores consolidated with other divisions. Six Hahne's stores consolidated with Lord & Taylor		
1990	Filed for bankruptcy. Reorganized $8B debt.	Acquired Thalhimers and Sibley's and consolidated with Kaufmann's	Investcorp acquired Saks & Co. from BAT PLC	
1991	Divisional consolidation began. Former Maas Brothers/Jordan Marsh stores operated under the Burdines name; division headquarters were consolidated.			
1992	A new public company (Federated Department Stores, Inc.) emerged. The former Allied Stores Corporation was merged into Federated; consolidation of the A&S and Jordan Marsh divisions.	Thalhimers consolidated with Hecht's. LS Ayres division consolidated with Famous-Barr.	Acquired 18 Hess stores (Southeast)	
1993		May Co. merged with Robinson's of LA; May Ohio consolidates with Kaufmann's; G.Fox consolidated with Fliene's; May D&F consolidated with Foley's.		
1994	Acquired R.H. Macy & Co., creating the largest department store retailer in the nation. Acquired the Joseph Horne Co. (10 stores in PA). Discontinued I.Magnin chain (131 I. Magnin stores sold or converted into Macy's or Bullock's).	Acquired 10 stores from Hess's of PA and NY.	Acquired 28 McRae's stores (Southeast); acquired 4 former I.Magnin stores.	
1995	Acquired LA-based Broadway Stores Inc. (included Emporium and Weinstock's). 56 stores were converted into Macy's, 5 became Bloomingdale. Rich's/Goldsmith's and Lazarus were consolidated into one division: Rich's/Lazarus/Goldsmith's.	Acquired 16 stores from Wanamaker and Woodward & Lathrop stores of DC and PA.	Acquired 3 Parks-Belk stores (TN)	
1996	Bullock's and Jordan Marsh stores renamed Macy's.	Acquired 13 Strawbridge & Clothier stores in PA.	Acquired 51 Younkers stores (Midwest); Acquired 38 Parisian stores (Southeast & Midwest)	

Year	Federated Department Stores	May Company	Saks Inc.	Dillards (private company)
1997			Acquired 40 Herberger's stores (Midwest & Great Plains)	
1998		Acquired 13 stores from Jone Stores.	Merged with Proffitt's Inc. Proffitt's corporate name changed to Saks Inc. Acquired 55 Carson Pirie Scott & Co. stores (Midwest); Acquired 6 Brody's stores (NC); 96 Saks Holdings (National)	Acquired Mercantile Stores
1999	Acquired Fingerhut Companies, Inc., a direct-marketing company.	Acquired 13 Zions Cooperative Mercantile Institution stores in Utah and Idaho, consolidated into Meier & Frank.		
2000		Acquired David's Bridal. Opened 123 new stores.		
2001	Federated Department Stores	May Company	Saks	Dillards
Month January		Purchased 9 Saks Inc. stores	Sold 9 stores to May Company	
February	Announced the closing of its Stern's division. Most locations to be converted into Bloomingdale's or Macy's.			Purchased 4 ZCMI stores from May Co.
March		Acquired 13 Montgomery Wards stores across the country		Purchased 8 Montgomery Wards
April				
May				
June	Acquired Liberty House (HI)			
July			Acquired 2 Montgomery Ward stores; closed Saks 5th Ave. store in White Plains NY; announced the elimination of its Foliio catalog operation.	

Sources: Individual company websites, Hoovers On-Line company capsules (www.hoovers.com)